THE BOOK OF
SHAUGH PARISH

It's a 'Shaugh' Thing

DON BALKWILL

HALSGROVE

First published in Great Britain in 2008

Copyright © 2008 Don Balkwill

British Library Cataloguing-in-Publication Data
A CIP record for this title is available from the British Library

ISBN 978 1 84114 694 2

HALSGROVE

Halsgrove House
Ryelands Industrial Estate
Bagley Road
Wellington
Somerset TA21 9PZ
T: 01823 653777
F: 01823 216796
e: sales@halsgrove.com
www.halsgrove.com

Frontispiece photograph: *Frank Lillicrap with Joyce
picking strawberries, 1952.*

Printed in Great Britain by CPI Antony Rowe Ltd, Wiltshire

CONTENTS

Acknowledgments

There have been so many people who, in so many ways, have contributed to this book. Without their assistance, *The Book of Shaugh Parish* would not have been possible, and I would like to thank all them for their help.

Those who contributed personal memories include:
Betty Norton, Bob Burns, Brian Willis, Celia Milne, Christine Bryan, David Naylor, David Tyrrell, David Tyrrell-Collins, Fred Winzor, Jeffrey Kellaway, Jill Sharpe, Joyce Butcher, Joyce Horsley, Justine Elder, Laurence Gibson, Len Webb, Linda Chatt, Malcolm Clarke, Malcolm Norman, Margaret Anstis, Margaret Blowey, Michael Waldron, Peter Ashton, Phil Kerswell, Rosalind May, Rosemary Harrison, Sarah Hugo, Ron Ayers, Sue Robinson, Susan Lyons, Tracey and Norman May. Memories of those no longer with us; Arthur D. Selleck, Gladdy Northmore, Jeffery Jones and Stan Brown.

Those who contributed photographs include:
Brian Willis, Bryan and Sue Pullyblank, Daniella Fry, David Andrew, Eddie Faulkner, Elaine and Roger Smerdon, Graham Eagle, Hazel Adams, David Tyrrell-Collins, Joyce Butcher, Laurence Gibson, Linda Chatt, Margaret Anstis, Margaret Blowey, John Partridge, Margaret Hugill, Margaret Roberts, Maureen Cook, Mrs R.J. Johnson, Mrs S.L. Richardson, Peter Ashton, Rachel Rayers, Ron Ayers, Rosalind May, Sue Robinson, Susan Lyons, Tracey and Norman May and William Daw.

Those who contributed factual material and drawings:
Brian Pundsack, Chris Titchener, Graham Eagle, John Partridge, Mark Howe, Sam Fry and Steve Roberts.

Those who provided help in identifying people places, dates, general encouragement and poetry:
Aisha Waldron, Amanda Cook, Barbara Bowles, Barry Isaacs, Bert Howells, Bill Phillips, Brian Randall, Brian Lear, Bryan L, Baker, Caroline Pitt, Claire Ashton, Claire Woods, Clive Deacon, Colin Batten, David Chamberlaine, David Compton, David Delag, Dawn Cawley, Denise Lyons, Diane Moyse, Eddie Doig, Elaine Elford, Elizabeth Ahir, Helen Jarvis, Helen Jones, Ian Lewis, James Ash, James Paxman, Jennie Winter, John and Annette Mungeam, John Abraham, John Hutchins, John and Janet Stitson, Julie Harmieson, Kay Titchener, Kelvin Butcher, Shaun Elder, Keith Ryan, Laura Robinson, Maggie Sutton, Malcolm Norman, Margaret Murdock, Michael and Carol Worledge, Mrs Faulkner, Pam and Barry Golding, Patricia Balkwill, Paul Rendell, Penny Meadows, Pippa Quelch, Rachel Rees, Rodney Hitchings, Roger Parsons, Frank and Sally Navarra, Sally Roberts, Sam and Pat Yeadon, Sarah Earl, Simon and Gill Goves, Simon Snelling, Simon Butler, Steve Roberts, Sue Ayers, Sue Burkill, Suzanne Lawrence, Tim Sandles, Tracey and Jim Elder, Vanessa Balkwill and, finally, my long-suffering and very supportive wife, Marilyn, without whose patience this book would have taken twice as long.

A special thankyou to the staff and pupils of Shaugh Prior Primary School, who put a lot of effort into hosting the afternoon when I visited and made all the visitors feel welcome. Also for working so hard on their drawings for the competition.

Thankyou everybody.

Introduction

The Parish of Shaugh is about eight miles north-east of Plymouth and runs from Shaugh Bridge at one end to Lee Moor at the other, with Shaugh Prior and Wotter in between. The area consists largely of moorland, rising to over 1,500 ft in places and is thickly dotted with remains of the Bronze Age. The parish is bounded on the north and west by the picturesque Plym Valley, especially beautiful at Shaugh Bridge, which is classed as part of the village of Shaugh Prior. The extensive china clay deposits at Lee Moor have been worked since the 1840s, and are now the most important source of the mineral in Devon.

The population of the three villages is around 500, living in just under 350 houses with a fairly even split between the three villages. Although only just over three miles from one end of the parish to the other, the contrast is almost unbelievable. Lee Moor and, to an extent, Wotter, have a bleak beauty with a barren white landscape, scarred and desolate, with spoil heaps from the local clay works that could make you think you are on the moon. In stark contrast, at the other end of the parish, Shaugh Bridge is a well-known beauty spot visited by thousands of walkers, climbers, fishermen and families throughout the year. With its meeting of two rivers overlooked by the craggy Dewerstone, it provides pleasure for all those who visit.

This is not a history of the Parish – most of that can be found elsewhere. Although there is some factual material, it is an unashamedly nostalgic return to the area, in words and pictures, by those who have lived, worked or visited here.

I didn't initially set out to write a book about the Parish of Shaugh; the idea sort of evolved over time. Whilst contemplating writing a book about Shaugh Prior Primary School I was given a number of old school photographs, together with a CD which contained lots of digital images of Shaugh and the surrounding area. About that time I found myself confined to the house for a couple of months because of back problems so to fill up my time I decided to create a website featuring most of the photographs, together with a number of my own. Within a very short space of time people began to provide me with other photographs, together with information about the history of the area and some of their own memories. The website grew over the next few months. More and more people contacted me, not only from the UK but from places as far flung as the USA, Canada, Australia and Botswana, most telling me how much they were enjoying the website. All had some sort of connection to the Shaugh area. Some had lived in the area, some had just visited and some had relatives who had lived here. Then it occurred to me, what happens when I can no longer keep the site updated, and what about all those older people who don't have access to the internet? After all, they are the people who would be most interested in old pictures. It was then I decided to put all the information on the website together in a book, and this is it. It would seem it is not uncommon for a book to evolve from a website or blog. Incidentally, I don't know when you will be reading this; it could be years in the future, so the website may no longer be in existence. However, if you want to see whether it is still out there these are the addresses: www.shaugh.net and www.memoriesofchildhood.co.uk I hope you enjoy the book as much as I did putting it together.

After writing this I suddenly realised that most of the memories and the pictures have been provided by people who no longer live in the parish. There must be something in the water that keeps drawing us back, or perhaps it's just that after you leave a place only then do you truly appreciate it. People have such fond memories of the area.

Talking of memories, please bear in mind that the mind can play tricks on all of us, so if you find any inaccuracies please don't get het up or angry about it, just bear in mind that this is not meant to be a factual history and that all the contributors provided their information as they remember it. Mistakes do happen. If I have inadvertently given photographs the wrong captions please forgive me. You too will grow old one day and your memory cells will start to disappear. I know because a lot of mine already have!

One final note. As I mentioned earlier, most of the photographs were given to me in digital form so in most cases I have no way of knowing who took them. I hope I haven't infringed anyone's copyright. If you recognise any of the photographs as being ones you took, let me know and I will be happy to withdraw them or acknowledge them in future reprints of the book. That's assuming, of course, there will be reprints!

Don Balkwill

Comments

What people said about the website www.shaugh.net

Julie Harmieson

Thank you so much for the history and general information on the site, it's brilliant. We have recently moved into the area and have been walking round the Dewerstone without knowing anything about it. I've searched the internet for info and your site was the only one that combined history, legend and personal memories. Thanks again.

Laura

What an interesting and informative site. My sister and I walk our dogs at Shaugh Bridge and have climbed up the Dewerstone (the safe way) for years. We also recently started cycling the Plym Valley Trail and that area and Shaugh Bridge have raised loads of questions for us, all of which have been answered here. This is one of the best sites I've visited and, what's more, written by someone who really knows the area, a rare thing and great to find. Thank you so much for sharing your memories and photographs.

Bob Burns - aged 64

This site has brought back a number of pleasant childhood memories of the area. Although I lived in Plymouth when I was a schoolboy, I knew the Shaugh area quite well, as my family visited the area by train or bus quite frequently. My mother (Ada Burns) was a good friend of Betty Waldron. During the summer school holidays in the 1950s we often spent a day with Betty and Arthur at Shaugh. Their son (Aisha's father) Michael was a few months older than me, and their daughter Sylvia was about the same age as my brother Allan. I still clearly remember descending the hill to Shaugh Bridge with the Waldron children and playing near the bridge and the Dewerstone. It is still one of my favourite places on the edge of Dartmoor.

Hamish Horton - aged 10

My gran is in the photo of the Shaugh School, her name is Una Horton but back then it would have been Pundsack. I go to Shaugh school now, my sister brother and dad and auntie went there too.

Aisha Waldron - aged 35

The little boy in your picture of Shaugh School is my father, Michael Louis Waldron. His father, Arthur William Waldron, was a member of the Parish Council and as I was informed was very involved with the parish and masons. He is in another of your pictures, 'Shaugh Parish Council 1951' and is the gentleman second from the left. He died the year after I was born, in 1973, and as a child visiting I remember keeping the grave tidy

with my grandmother, Bessie Amelia Waldron, and also polishing the brass plate on the original gates into the church. This is a lovely site and has also given me some fond memories of my visits as a child.

Len Webb - aged 62

In the 1950s our Scout troop camped in a field near the village. Our group scoutmaster had connections with the area. We were taken down a shaft called Drakes Dyke, which was the old water supply for Plymouth. All I can remember was that it was dark, wet and a long way underground.

Malcolm Clarke - aged 60

Well done Don, the site is developing really well. I was next door neighbour to David and Michael Tyrell in the 1950s and, along with Raymond Jenkins and you, attended Plympton Grammar School with Phil Kerswell and many others. I was better known as Nobby Clarke, as were my older brothers.

Phil Kerswell - aged 62

I was brought up and went to school in Lee Moor. Just going through your messages I went to Plympton Grammar with Glyn Jones. 'Twould be nice to chat with others of that era.

I now live in Botswana but try to come back every couple of years and have a pint in the White Thorn. Hope to hear from somebody.

Sarah Hugo - aged 52

A really interesting site and unfortunately I can't immediately recognise anyone at the school either. Having lived in the Lee Moor/Shaugh area in the late '50s/early '60s the Post Office was definitely in use at the time I left in 1966 (the postmistress's name was Mrs Manville, I think).

Helen Jones

Just wanted to say how nice it was to look through the photos. My dad (Glyn Jones) and his family used to live in one of those huts! He has always told me stories about growing up and I've visited the areas many times, but it's great to see old photos as he has none. Thanks for putting this together,

Claire Ashton

Wow! This is great. My family will be very interested in your site and history. We have a special connection with the Goodameavy area of the Dewerstone. My grandfather brought his family there from Plymouth during the war and built a hut near the river, where they lived. Later the hut was replaced with a caravan on the other side of the river and we spent many happy days there in my own childhood. My father and his sister knew the Leggs from the cottage. We have some photos that you may like. I will forward your details on to my Dad. Would be lovely to meet you and exchange stories!

Sue Robinson, Canada - aged 38
Great site! My Dad's family came from Shaugh - great-grandfather helped build the bridge, great-aunt taught at the school, etc. So this is very interesting to see!

Suzanne Lawrence
What an interesting site! I loved the old school photos. My husband's family all came from the area for generations and I bet some of those children are related to him. Some of his family names are Baskerville, Luscombe, Skelley and Mattacott. A lot of his family are buried in the churchyard. Thanks for all the lovely background info.

David Tyrrell - aged 66
Great work on the website. With some very interesting links. Having studied the school photographs for the period I attended, I was perplexed that not only could I not recognise my old school mates; I could not even recognise myself! A fat lot of good I would be on 'Friends Reunited'.

Roger Parsons - aged 61
As I also lived and attended school at Shaugh it is wonderful that someone has put together such memories.
    Thanks from Australia

Jennie Winter - aged 35
A wonderful website. Having grown up in Shaugh Prior it is lovely to see someone taking such an interest in the area and compiling so many resources for others to enjoy. Keep up the good work, I'll be checking in on the site to keep abreast of updates.

Amanda Cook
What a wonderful website, with great content. It is so thoughtful of you to have taken the time to share your memories with so many others. I know that this was done for your grandchildren but I'm sure that this will benefit many other children too.

Sally Navarra
You have done an outstanding job with this project, and I love visiting the area via your pictures. Perhaps one day Frank and I will be able to make the trip to see you and Marilyn and your beautiful country. Until then keep up the good work. Now get back to that washing and ironing!!
    Sally and Frank, your USA travel buddies

Brian Longland
Heard about your website on Radio Devon. Well done on producing such an informative and well-presented site. I'll certainly keep coming back to see your latest updates. Congratulations on all your hard work.

Left: *A very early greetings card from Shaugh Prior.*

Gorse Cottage, Shaugh Prior, in a painting dating from 1909. The building on the far right is the old church school, although, with artistic licence, it appears closer to the next building than it actually avvas.

CHAPTER 1

Shaugh Prior

Shaugh Prior is very picturesque, and there are excellent views over Plymouth Sound and across to Cornwall. There are a number of ancient farms scattered about the parish, some of which are recorded in the Doomsday Book. The centre of the village has a church, St Edwards, a pub, the White Thorn, a County Primary School and about 17 cottages and houses. There used to be a Post Office but that closed in the mid-1950s

Stan Brown

Sadly Stan is no longer with us, but fortunately he wrote down his recollections of earlier times which originally appeared in the Parish Magazine in 1993.

I remember Shaugh Prior when there were only 23 dwellings. Now that number has tripled. It was a village of kind and gentle men, Mr Harold Kennard, Mr George Hilson, Mr Bill Lillicrap, Mr Fred Jeffries, Mr Charlie Lee, Mr Walter Belsher and the vicar, the Revd Ralph Alexander, who all had time to stop and talk to children.

There was always movement of local people in the village during the day, not faces behind windscreens that left in the morning and returned at night or week-ends, and the only dialect heard was Devonshire.

I think at that time, say 1929, there were only four cars in the village. All the farm transport was horse-drawn; the Revd Alexander had a donkey and jingle

(trap). Every Saturday morning horses and traps would leave the farms in the area taking farmers' wives to Shaugh Station en route to Plymouth with dairy produce to sell in the pannier market.

Mr Tom Selleck from Wotter Farm was the dairyman for Shaugh Prior, making deliveries with horse and milk float. I remember the present White Thorn Inn being built. Previously on the site had stood a cart shed for Under Shaugh Farm. The old White Thorn standing nearby was very much alive as the local inn (the only one for Shaugh Prior, Wotter and Lee Moor). The Moorland Hotel, then the Moorland Guest House, was purely residential.

The church was a very important part of our childhood. Every child in the village went to Sunday school at 10.15a.m. then remained for matins at 11.00a.m. to sing in the choir, and then back again for Evensong at 6.30p.m.

I remember being reprimanded by the Revd Alexander during Sunday school with a sharp tap on the head from a large hymn book. That evening, just before Evensong, I saw him descend into the boiler house to stoke the boiler. Remembering that sharp blow on the head I promptly closed the hatch door, locking him in, then ran away. Compassion quickly took over. I ran back to unlock the hatch and ran into the vestry. I was pulling my surplice over my head when the Revd Alexander came in 'puffing a little'. My face was still covered by my surplice as he placed his hand on my

The farmhouse below the church tower is Under Shaugh Farm, now called Upper Shaugh Farm! The track is the original road to Shaugh Bridge, c.1909.

Nos 1 and 2 Spring Cottages, c.1950.

Bill Lillicrap and mates during the First World War.

Above: *Bill, George, Ida and Annie Lillicrap.*

Left: *Bill Lillicrap with George and Annie Lillicrap outside Spring Cottage.*

Frank, George and Annie Lillicrap.

Frank and Winifred Lillicrap, 1931.

shoulder and said, 'Stanley, I'm sorry about this morning', and the subject was closed. Truly a saintly man,
whom I remember with great love and respect. It was
several years later that he died. In fact the day before, I
was kindly invited to assist in the Second World War.

Stan Brown was married to Doreen Brown. They
lived in a cottage near the mill with his parents, Stan
and Edna, who had the kiosk at Shaugh Bridge.
Later their daughter, Edna Kellaway, took over and
ran the kiosk for many years before selling it.

Joyce Butcher, née Lillicrap

*I lived at No. 2 Spring Cottages and my grandparents,
Dad's parents, lived in No 1.*

*Dad used to grow all our vegetables – potatoes, peas,
beans, cabbage, carrots. We would store the potatoes in
an earth and straw cave; they would keep for months.
We had fruit trees – apple, plum, raspberries, goose-
berry and strawberries. Mum would make jam and
bottle some of the fruit for the winter.*

*Granddad Lillicrap used to keep his horses in the field
opposite Spring Cottages.*

Reg and Mary Jarvis with their son Desmond sitting on the mound outside Spring Cottage.

Joyce Lillicrap in her Guide uniform outside Spring Cottage, c.1960.

George and Annie Lillicrap were my grandparents.

Bill (William) Lillicrap was their son and is my Dad's brother and my uncle. He married Ida.

Mary Jarvis was their daughter, my Dad's sister and my aunt. Desmond Jarvis was son of Reg Jarvis and Frank Lillicrap was their other son. He is my father and he married Winifred, my mother.

I went to Shaugh Primary School, and used to walk up the hill every day. I remember having cheese and potato pie for lunch; to this day I do not eat cheese!

Mrs Armistead used to give us her apple skin, which she peeled from an apple in one long piece! Happy days!

I joined the church choir and went every Sunday twice a day, and also to Sunday school, so I had to walk up the hill three times on a Sunday.

My Sunday lunchtime treat was to be allowed to buy a bottle of Applecham from Mrs Kellaway's shop at Shaugh Bridge.

We used to play down by the river, have picnics, and paddle in the water. We also played up on the moors opposite Mrs Kingwell's – football with the boys and games with the girls. I think it was only me and Margaret Parsons, the rest were boys.

Mum and I would catch the train from Shaugh Bridge to go shopping in Plymouth, and Dad would go and watch Plymouth Argyle play football. Sometimes we'd walk up the hill to catch the bus from Shaugh Prior.

Granddad worked at the clay works at Shaugh Bridge. I was told Dad also did for a while, but I only remember him working at Watts Blake, Cadover Bridge. If it snowed he had to walk all the way there and back, however sometimes a Land Rover would collect him, and if the snow was really bad he would stay at work for a few days.

My mother's parents and sisters lived in Dartmoor Cottage in Wotter, so in school holidays I would spend time there – I would ride my bike and Mum would walk, or catch the bus. In Wotter we used to play with my cousins and friends, football and tennis in the old clay settling pits, or ride our bikes on the sand tips. I went to the Girl Guides on a Monday evening in the hall under the chapel; Mrs Stacey was the Guide mistress. I had piano lessons after school at Lee Moor School with Miss Cann. She would tap your knuckles with a ruler if you got the notes wrong!

Gladdy Northmore

The following article appeared in the Parish magazine in 1993. Although Gladdy Northmore is no longer with us, her daughter, Joyce Quest, gave permission for it to be used in the book:

I well remember in the late 1920s the dances were held up Huxton Farm on a Saturday night, in one of the barns, lit by lanterns and oil lamps. The barn was well brushed and clean, whitewashed, and then decorated with greenery and balloons by the daughters of Mr and Mrs Lillicrap, who then lived at Huxton. The girls were helped by two or three willing lads who were eager to come to the dances.

We all used to have a marvellous time as there was always a good crowd from the three villages and Cornwood, with also boys and maids from Meavy and Sheepstor. We would get there by Shanks's pony, by bicycle or on horseback.

The dance would start at about eight o'clock with Mrs Marion Edwards from Mount Clogg Farm playing the piano, and it would finish at midnight. By that time the lamps and lanterns would be running out of oil, so in the darkness we would be searching for our shoes and boots under the benches. Some of the boys and lads came in their hobnailed boots and the girls in their walking shoes or boots, then change into their dancing shoes. Some lads would put on black patent shoes. When it was time to get our shoes, sometimes we could only find one of our own and one on someone else's as

St Edward's Church, 2007. Inset: *The fifteenth-century font cover rescued from a storage shed in the 1870s.*

A Sunday charabanc outing from Shaugh Prior, c.1930.

The Vicarage, Shaugh Prior.

one of the boys had either mixed them up or hid it for fun. What a laugh to try to find the right one! But they were happy days.

I married in the year 1934 and came to live at Huxton Farm myself. The dances were then held in the hut (Village Hall), as we called it. The pianist was Mrs Balkwill from Cornwood. We had some good times there. As time went on the hut gradually improved through the hard work of the different committees raising money. Over all these years they have worked very hard indeed to make the Village

Hall a lovely place with all its modern and up-to-date facilities and I am glad that the Hall is well patronised and used.

St Edward's Church

St Edward's Church is named after King Edward, who was born in AD961 and crowned King of England in 975 at the tender age of 14 years. The original Shaugh Prior church was built in the twelfth century. However, this must have been demolished

St Edward's Parish Church Officers, c.1930.

Above, left and right: *Flower Festival, 1969.*

Above and below: *The interior of the church, 2007.*

Shaugh Prior village centre, c.1930.

The Post Office and church, c.1936.

font cover that was rescued from a storage shed in the 1870s and restored. Parish registers going back to 1565 are held in the Devon Record Office, so it has been around a while and is the oldest building in the village. Not being a churchgoer myself I cannot tell you any more than you can read in the history books and on the internet.

The Post Office was situated in the village centre right next to the steps leading up to the church and opposite the old White Thorn. It can be seen in many of the postcards of the pre-'50s era. However, the history goes back much further. According to the records, in 1870 a Miss Sarah Belcher came to the village of Shaugh Prior as teacher and postmistress. On 10 August 1896 a date stamp was issued for the village as a sub-office under Plymouth.

In 1908 a date stamp was in use showing it as a sub-office under Roborough.

In 1914 the records still show that the sub-post-mistress was still Miss Sarah Belcher (shopkeeper). Letters went via Roborough. The nearest Money Order Office was at Lee Moor and the Telegraph Office was at Bickleigh Railway Station. This Post Office closed in the '50s, the last postmistress being a Miss Manley. (According to one quote she was 'a miserable old bat'.) Martin Harris ran the Post Office much later from his small grocery shop (with delivery service) which also doubled as a watch mending/engraving business a bit further down in the village.

Michael Waldron (aged 65)

My name is Michael Waldron and my parents moved to Shaugh towards the end of the war when I was 4–5 years old. We lived in the village at 'Ivydene'. I used to go fishing down at the river and get sweets from

at some point as the current church is a fifteenth-century granite building with a fine west tower. In the church there is a remarkable fifteenth-century

The cottage became a small grocery shop.

Mrs Kellaway at the little shack shop. I also had a sister, Sylvia.

I remember the camp down in the woods was referred to as 'The Colony' by those in the village (not always favorably). I did go there to tea at a friend's but I cannot remember who. There were also two brothers who I think used to poach the salmon.

I also remember Mrs Tottle and others. I remember Paul Harding [the Hardings were pet shop owners on Mutley Plain] and myself lighting a bonfire and putting old tins of spaghetti from his Dad's shed on it... 'Bang!' Spaghetti everywhere. The tortoises used to arrive in big teachests covered in ticks [the tortoises, not the tea chests! DB]. I also remember his sister, Gillian – had a bit of a crush on her. The Kingwells, Ralph, Jill and Judy, lived at the top of Shaugh Hill. The two sisters pinched my trousers once on the moor, although I did try to resist. I used to walk with my mum to the station to go shopping on a Saturday in Plymouth. Luckily Dad would pick us up at my Aunt Kit's in Plymouth so did not have to walk back up the hill. On another note (pun intended), I remember the rock and roll and twisting in the Village Hall at Shaugh 'Beat Night' with resident DJ on the Dansette.

I sang in the church choir along with my dad and sister, and we used to ring the bells. Dad was an ardent campanologist and I did have a go on the treble bell at one time. I also remember my first trip up the church tower – scary.

I remember Brian and Mervyn Pundsack and their sister Una, but I don't recall anything about Brian's accident [see page 91]. I remember we all used to

The elderly lady (centre) *is Dorothy English, wife of Captain Oswald English who lived at Cross gates in 1949. The little boy on the right is Bryan Pullyblank.*

congregate down at the bridge on a Saturday and Sunday. Some mates used to come out from Plymouth and stay down in the woods somewhere. I had a motor-cycle and sidecar, which did give me a bit of an advantage with the opposite gender. We were not very kind to the Scouts camping out under the Dewerstone, as I recall, and I liked to spend a lot of time fishing in the river and did once have to scoot because the local PC's helmet appeared over the horizon. I used to walk up the hill regularly when I went fishing down at the river (garden worms for bait, some nice trout and eels) until I got caught by the river bailiff, who showed me how to fly fish. Funny, I never caught anything after that. After Shaugh I went on to Plympton Grammar and my sister to the secondary modern there.

After schooling I took up psychiatric nursing at Moorhaven Hospital, Biddeford. I moved to Somerset and worked at the Mendip Hospital until they closed it in 1991, when I moved into the private nursing home sector. I married and had three children, one boy, two girls. I got divorced after 35 plus years. I retired and moved to North Wales and remarried Rieghan, who I met on the internet.

I do some fishing in the sea around here, which gets me out of the house and provides supper if I am lucky. I do a little woodcarving when the weather is warm and have written some poetry and the odd children's story, but no big publications.

The White Thorn Inn

The current White Thorn Inn was built on the site of an old cart shed in the early 1930s. Prior to the current building being constructed there was the Old White Thorn Inn, a much smaller building a few yards away, which is now a private house. The age of this building is uncertain but it is known that when churches were being built inns were often built at the same time to house the workmen carrying out the construction work. Whether this is the case at Shaugh is unknown. What is known is that the inn had a peat fire. In the days when peat was used as a domestic fuel it was not uncommon for the fire to be

Top and above: *Old views of the village.*

The White Thorn Inn, 2007.

kept burning in the hearth for years on end. It was recorded in 1873 that a peat fire had been kept burning in the White Thorn since 1833 without going out once! (It's amazing what lengths some people will go to not have to lay the fire on a cold winter's morning, isn't it?) The last landlord, or I should say landlady, of the the Old White Thorn was a Mrs Harris.

There have been quite a number of landlords of the new White Thorn since it was built, none of whom, it would seem, could make a success of the pub. At the end of the Second World war a Lt-Col. Arthur W.S. Gibson of the Royal Engineers, aged 60 at the time, became the landlord for 2–3 years. Unfortunately he lost a lot of money, like a number of the others, and moved out. At the time of writing the proprietors are Will and Nicky Lord; hopefully they can make a success of the place.

Laurence Gibson (aged 61)

The photograph of the British Legion in 1947 (overleaf) shows my father pretty well exactly in the middle – the balding gent with round glasses and a few medals. His name was Lt-Col. Arthur W.S. Gibson of the Royal Engineers – the medals are two First World War campaign medals (commonly known, I believe, as 'Mutt

Lawrence Gibson's christening, 31 August 1947.

Above: *Shaugh Prior British Legion, 1947.*

Lt-Col Arthur W.S. Gibson, landlord of the White Thorn, with sons David and Bill, 1947 .

and Geoff'); the third (cross-shaped) medal is the military OBE. He was aged about 60 at the time of the photograph.

My parents were landlords (or strictly, tenants) of the White Thorn for two to three years around this time, and I was born there in 1947. My mother was Emily, often known as Emma (née Ashton) and she was considerably younger than my father, having been born in 1909. Their business at the pub was not a success, and they lost quite a lot of money. After leaving Shaugh my father worked for some years as a surveyor/draftsman at one of the Army barracks at Crownhill.

I was christened at Shaugh on 31 August 1947. According to my baptismal certificate, the vicar was Frank Rider. One shows me with my mother and the other the whole family – my eldest brother is David; the middle brother is William, usually known at that time as Bill George. Someone might recognise the location – the gate itself will have long gone, but the gateway and the rocks may not have changed! Bill attended Shaugh school during our time there, but David went away to a prep school.

CHAPTER 2

Shaugh Prior County Primary School

Shaugh Prior CP was my first school. It's not changed much in over 50 years except that it now has an extension and inside toilets, which it didn't have in my day. I started school on 7 September 1950. How can I be so precise? I've seen, and have a copy of, the original register. The school itself was built in 1881. The school was, and still is, very small. You walk through the entrance foyer into the corridor. It still has the children's coat hooks on the left-hand wall. As you go down the corridor, the door on the right led into the infant classroom, and the door on the left led to the junior classroom. The junior classroom doubled as the dining-room because the kitchens are on the far side of this classroom. There was, and still is, a hatch in the far wall through which school dinners are served. The total number of children in the school varied between 30 and 50. I attended the school from 1950 to 1956. My first memory of the school is my very first day. My mother took me to the school and tried to leave me. I screamed and screamed, I suppose because I was scared. I had had no experience of interaction with other children at that stage. I was hanging on to my mother and pleading with her not to leave me. Of course she had to, and eventually I was dragged into

class. Whether we were told then what the rules for going to the toilet were, or whether my mother had told me previously, I don't know. What I do know is that later in the morning I put my hand up to go to the toilet and was given permission. Instead of going to the toilets, which were outside, I proceeded to do a runner and went home. My mother, of course, took me back to school again. I don't know whether I was punished for escaping, but I rather think not because I have no memory of it. I now have very fond memories of the two teachers there, Mrs Nelmes, the infant teacher, and Mrs Armistead, who taught the juniors and was also the headmistress.

The following entries for head teachers and teachers at Shaugh Prior Schools since they opened in 1873 are taken from Kelly's and White's directories and can be a little confusing.

The 1873 entry in the Post Office Directory, edited by Kelly, states: 'There is a small church school'.

The school was called the National School and Miss Elizabeth Priest was named as the first schoolmistress

The School Board, consisting of five members, was formed on 6 November or 28 December 1874, depending on which directory you look at, and

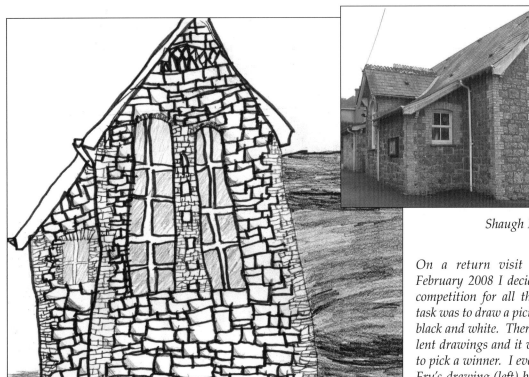

Shaugh Prior School, 2008.

On a return visit to the school in February 2008 I decided to hold a little competition for all the children. Their task was to draw a picture of the school in black and white. There were many excellent drawings and it was difficult for me to pick a winner. I eventually chose Sam Fry's drawing (left) because of the detail involved.

Shaugh Prior CP School football team sometime during Eric Anstis's reign. On the left is Bert Ryder and on the right Eric Anstis, the head of Shaugh School. Adrian Langford is the tall boy in the centre at the back and either side of him are Alan Phillips and Ian Wall.

consisted of the Sir Massey Lopes, Bart (chairman) and Revd G.R. Scobel (vice-chairman and honorary clerk), together with Messrs Martin, Mattacott and Andrews.

In 1878 Kelly shows the National School mistress as Miss Laura Preece, while in another directory a Miss Giles is named as schoolmistress. In 1881 the current County Primary School opened. In 1883 an entry for the National School shows Miss Lavinia Vosper as schoolmistress

By 1889 the clerk to the board was James Bettes of Lee Moor. The school had 70 children on roll, with an average attendance of 46. Miss Sarah Belcher was schoolmistress. By 1890 she was also listed as sub-postmistress of Shaugh Prior.

Also in 1890 the Board School of Lee Moor had a schoolmistress called Mrs Sarah Bettes, possibly the wife of the clerk, James Bettes. Lee Moor is in the parish of Shaugh Prior and was growing at this time because the production of china clay was expanding.

The attendance was the same in 1893 but the schoolmistress was by now a Miss Elizabeth Harris. Sarah Belcher was still listed as sub-postmistress for Shaugh Prior.

The Board School in Lee Moor, a mixed school for

120 children, had an average attendance of 90, and Mrs Sarah Bettes was still the schoolmistress.

In 1902 Shaugh Prior average attendance had dropped to 38 and a Miss Mary Jenkins was the schoolmistress. On the other hand, Lee Moor Board School now had 180 children with an average attendance of 110. Guess who was the schoolmistress? Got it in one – Mrs Sarah Bettes.

In 1910 the schools were controlled by six managers. Shaugh Prior average attendance had risen to 40 and a Miss Wager was schoolmistress. Lee Moor's average attendance was down to 96 and Mrs Sarah Bettes was still there. It appears she stayed there until 1926, a total of 36 years. The schoolmistress at Shaugh Prior was a Mrs Cork in 1914 and a Mrs Hooper in 1919. She stayed until 1926, when Mrs Williams became schoolmistress of Shaugh Prior and a Mr Edward J. Hathaway was schoolmaster at Lee Moor.

The School Board seems to have been quite progressive for its time because until the Sex Disqualification (Removal) Act was passed in 1919 all female teachers were supposed to be single. This Act made it unlawful to disqualify anyone on the grounds of sex or marriage from holding a public

Shaugh County Primary School Over the Years

Shaugh Prior School, c.1921.

The school in the 1930s. Left right, back row: M. Skidmore, J. Elford, T. May, W. Kennard, P. Kennard, L. Vincent, S. May, P. Blackler, ? Pundsack; middle row: S. Pullyblank, J. Kingwell, R. Walke, P. Lee, A. Lillicrap., ? Peek, E. Tucker, F. Kingwell, D. Doidge, I. Peek; front row: A. Damerell, A. Kingwell, P. Elford, E. Pullyblank, C. Trethewey, I. Pullyblank.

Shaugh County Primary School Over the Years

With teachers Mrs Williams and Miss W. Jeffery, c.1933/34.

The school, c.1935.

Shaugh County Primary School Over the Years

The school, c.1936.

The school, c.1937.

The school c.1939.

Shaugh County Primary School Over the Years

Shaugh County Primary School Over the Years

The school in 1940.

The school in 1948.

Shaugh Prior School, c.1957. Left to right, back row: *Mrs Dyer, Clive Pundsack, Malcolm Clarke, Leslie Quirke, Roger Andrews, Roger Parsons, Hendrick Luckett, David Kennard, ?, David Fookes, Mrs Nelmes;* third row: *Mrs Legg, Linda Walters, Hazel Damerell, Sylvia Waldron, Margaret Parsons, Joyce Lillicrap, Lorna Pundsack, Pauline May, Jean Vincent, Jennifer Ball, Margaret Vanstone, Mrs Armistead;* second row: *Jean Ball, Jean Damerell, Sandra Jellyman, ?, ?, ?, Wendy Chambers, Jill Jutson;* front row: *Leonard Ball, Francis Kinsman, Timothy Chisholm, Justine Balkwill, Brendan Coombes, Susan Walke, Jeffery Kellaway, ?, ?.*

function. Although, before that time, married women had not been allowed to work as teachers, Shaugh School Board had employed female married teachers since 1889.

The Act should, in theory, have meant greater equality for women entering the teaching profession, but in the 1920s working women were frowned upon as there were so many men on the dole.

For example, some authorities still refused to employ married women as teachers. This rule meant that if a woman teacher got married, she had to resign from her job; if she didn't she was sacked.

Unfortunately, there is no reference to either school in the directories from 1930 to 1939. However, we know from Joyce Elliott and her elder sister, Molly, that Mrs Williams was head teacher until 1939. They were taught by a Miss Chislett and by a Miss Winifred Jeffery, who married on 2 October 1932 and whose father was Fred Jeffery (see Chapter 7).

In 1939 Miss Joan Alford took over the headship of Shaugh School and stayed for nine years. A Miss Hughes also taught at the school, as did a Miss Skerrett. Fortunately, the 1919 Act meant that female teachers were no longer forced to leave their jobs on marriage, so Mrs Armistead was able to secure the

post of head teacher in 1948. She stayed until 1962. During that time Mrs Nelmes also taught at the school.

The first male head was Mr Eric Anstis, who took over in 1962. He remained in situ for 16 years, until 1978. Mrs Nelmes taught until about 1964, when she retired. Her place was taken by Mrs Maureen Cook in 1965/66. After Mr Anstis there were a number of temporary heads: Tony Butler (1982), Les Tracy, Jean Aldersley (1989), Avril Popplestone (1989)

Then in 1995 came Miss Caroline Pitt, who is the incumbent at the time of writing.

Eric Edwin Anstis, Headmaster 1962–1978
(provided by Margaret Anstis - aged 87)

Eric Anstis was born in Townsend Avenue, Ford, Plymouth, on 10 August 1921 and educated at Ford Primary School and Sutton High School. He was a talented boy chorister, much in demand at local churches and concerts.

He joined the City Treasury in 1937, working in the tax office; he also joined the Territorial Army (Devon Heavy Regt RA) that year. He was called to the colours in August 1939 and served at Western

Shaugh Prior School, c.1980. Included in the photograph are: *Steven Vincent, Gary Brown, Lee Bowden, Kim Brown, Marie Howard, John Stone, Paul Hayes, Adrian Stoker, Darren Hayes, Katherine Pearce, John Carthew, Rachel Walters, Nicholas Daw, Gary Andrew, Kim Stratton, Nicola Brazier, Mark Clinic, James ?, Steven Tucker, Peter Goss, Dawn Rowland, Christopher Rowland, Sarah Kingwell, Richard Taylor, Mandy Gregor, Shaun Andrew, Jason McGrath, Rachel Rayers, Lisa Snow, Mrs Byrne, Tony Butler (head), Miss Coyle, N. Best, Janice Taylor, Anthony Howard, Hayley McCullum, Susan Pearce, Scott Hayes, Julie Weaver, Lisa Brazier, Diane Carthew, Nigel Clegg, Scott Bowden.*

Probably a sports day where all the parents were invited, c.1952.

The school c.1947, including Gordon Kellaway; Martin Parsons, Ken Clarke, John Kennard, Michael Waldron, John May, David Phillips, Ralph Kingwell, David May, Bill Lillicrap, Roy Lillicrap, Bryan Pullyblank, Stuart May.

Kings and in the Orkney Islands. He became a sergeant at 19 and was commissioned in 1942 into the Field Artillery. He took part in the invasion of Europe from D-Day+1 to his demob in 1946.

He married Margaret Ford in 1943 in St Jude's Church, Plymouth, where they had both been keen members of the youth section. His first son, Neil, was born in 1945.

On leaving the Army Eric briefly returned to the City Treasury but in 1948 he started his teaching career at Redland Training College, Bristol. His second son, Paul, was born in 1947. Eric's first teaching post was at Little Green Primary School in Croxley Green, Hertfordshire. He then returned to Devon with his wife and two sons, taking a post at Goosewell Primary School, Plymstock. His third son, Alan, was born in 1952.

From 1952 to 1960 he served in the Territorial Army, becoming CO with the rank of Major of the 57 (M) Signal Regiment TA, based at Crownhill Fort. He was instrumental in launching a very successful recruiting campaign during this period and the membership of the TA was drastically increased. He was an extremely popular leader and the family has received many messages from past members of the TA acknowledging this.

In 1956 he became headmaster of Lee Mill County Primary School, near Ivybridge. In 1962 he became headmaster at Shaugh Prior County Primary School, where he remained until ill health forced his retirement in 1978. During this period he took a year's study leave and gained an Advanced Diploma in Education with distinction at Cambridge. He also ran the Ivybridge Teachers' Centre, a radical new idea to help young teachers in particular, but also to provide established teachers with any advice or aids they may require.

He was highly respected and greatly loved by all the children he taught. He catered not only to all their academic needs, but was driven by a desire to make them grow into happy, well adjusted, honest and worthy citizens.

He loved and respected everyone he met, always looking for the good in everything around him. He influenced so many people with his gentle, loving and humorous manner. He was a scholar and a gentleman in every way. His sense of humour came into all he did, but it was never cruel or hurtful. He always looked at things from the other person's point of view.

He had a great sense of fairness and justice. In his TA days as CO of the Signals Regiment, they christened him 'The Thinker', as he always answered 'I'll think about that' before rushing into anything.

In 1978 he and Margaret moved to Yelverton and he became an enthusiastic member of Yelverton Golf Club, thoroughly enjoying the sport and the companionship he found there. He was an enthusiastic member of the veterans' section.

He loved the simple pleasures in life and to be surrounded by the family and friends who meant so much to him. He was very proud of his sons and his grandchildren, without realising how much he was responsible for their success.

His funeral took place on Monday, 19 October 1998 and was conducted by the Revd Richard Tebbs at St Paul's Church, Yelverton. The church was crowded and a personal tribute was given by each of his sons, Neil, Paul and Alan.

Sarah Hugo (aged 52)

As a child I lived in Wotter (1956–58), Lee Moor (1958–64) and Shaugh (1964–66), going first to Lee Moor and then to Shaugh Prior school. I had one term in the infants just before Mrs Nelmes retired and then went to the juniors under Eric Anstis before my family moved to the Bath/Bristol area.

I remember during the summer months quite frequently going to Shaugh Bridge with a couple of my peers (no grown-ups) to spend an afternoon swinging on the ropes and generally messing around (probably have to call Social Services these days).

David Tyrrell (aged 66)

These are some of my memories of Shaugh Prior School. It is a bit sketchy as my memory is notoriously poor! I can't even remember the names of my classmates.

I started at Shaugh School in about 1948/49, when we moved from Plympton up to Wotter, and left in 1953 after taking the 11+ and moving on to Plympton Secondary Modern.

In those days we lived in a bungalow called Byways, at the end of Collard Lane, Wotter. I used to walk the mile or so to school from home, up the lane and over the moor, on my own to start with, then meeting up with some of the Wotter lads on the way. Can you imagine letting infants do that nowadays?

Journeys to and from school were made more interesting by having a quick game of football or cricket, depending on the season, on the 'bowling green', which was just to the west of Beatland Corner. Sometimes we came across the Commandos from Bickleigh on training exercises, running backwards up the steep hills with full packs on. They would often let us carry their guns for them, which I assume were not loaded at the time! If we were lucky, one of us had been able to get hold of some matches to set fire to a gorse bush or make a pretend camp fire.

Children in the playground, c.1965.

On arrival at Shaugh Prior, before going into the school, we often would go to the shop by the church with our ration book to buy a few pence worth of sweets, sherbet dabs, or if we were flush, a Wagon Wheel. Many times on getting to the school we were soaking wet so clothes were put to dry on the guard round the big coke-fired stove that dominated the main classroom.

My memory of the actual lessons is very poor. Perhaps if I had paid more attention I would have remembered more and passed to go to the Grammar School in Plympton, my failure to do so being of great disappointment to my parents, as my Mother was secretary there!

I can remember Mrs Armistead well and I can remember sitting in a semicircle round the stove calling out our times tables parrot fashion. Music lessons stick in my mind, as even at that tender age I had a very tuneless singing voice. I was therefore asked not to be in the choir but to stand beside the pianist and turn the sheet music for her whilst keeping quiet.

One of the highlights for me was during the summer term, on very warm days; we would take our desks out to the playground and have our lessons in the open air. This had the benefit of giving me even more distractions, as from a very early age I had more interest in nature than academics. I could therefore gaze at the birds or the farmers working in the fields and let the subject being taught sail right over my head.

Every day the canteen produced a cooked meal for us,

School manager (governor) Mrs Hetty Trethewey, Mr John Cobbledick Selleck (far right) and Mrs Armistead (at the piano).

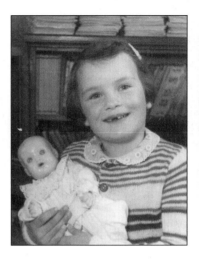

From left: *Bryan Pullyblank 1949; Michael Waldron; Susan Walke; the author at his desk, c.1955.*

On the grass, c.1952.

Swimming lessons at Cadover Bridge, c.1965.

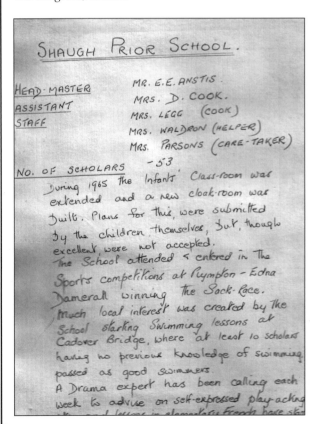

SHAUGH PRIOR SCHOOL.

HEAD-MASTER   MR. E.E. ANSTIS.
ASSISTANT   MRS. D. COOK.
STAFF   MRS. LEGG (COOK)
   MRS. WALDRON (HELPER)
   MRS. PARSONS (CARE-TAKER)

NO. OF SCHOLARS   -53.
During 1965 the Infants' Class-room was
extended and a new cloak-room was
built. Plans for this, were submitted
by the children themselves, but, though
excellent were not accepted.
The School attended & entered in the
Sports competitions at Plympton - Edna
Damerall winning the Sack-Race.
Much local interest was created by the
School starting Swimming lessons at
Cadover Bridge, where at least 10 scholars
having no previous knowledge of swimming
passed as good swimmers.
A Drama expert has been calling each
week to advise on self-expressed play-acting

Above: *Pauline and Margaret May, c.1955.*

Left: *Extract from a journal detailing the school's progress in 1965.*

The retirement of Mrs Parsons, the caretaker, c.1982.

which mostly I wolfed down in order to be able to get out into the playground to play football or five stones. However, I can recall one day when I refused to eat the tapioca that I was made to sit there until I did. By the end of the lunch break I was still there and the table was needed for lessons so I thought I had won as they took the still full dish away, until I had to take a note home to my parents describing my disruptive behavior.

Another memory that has stuck with me is of the whole school sitting in a big circle in the playground whilst someone very sadly announced that the king had died and we should say prayers. We were then told that Princess Elizabeth would become queen.

I now live in Horrabridge [2008]. Only about four or five miles from where I was brought up, but in the intervening years I have lived mainly away from Devon. When we moved here, one of the neighbours, on learning my background, asked if I had come home to die. I replied, 'Yes, but hopefully not yet!'

On leaving Plympton Secondary Modern I went into farming and attended Bicton Agricultural College and then had various jobs on farms in the south of England. Becoming disillusioned with my inability to get my own farm, I moved out of farming and, after a few false starts, found my niche in the life assurance industry.

After a successful period in life assurance sales, I

moved into sales management, and then, within the head office of one of the UK's largest insurance companies, I became involved in strategic and change management. I finally retired at 58 as the sales and marketing director of a Birmingham-based mutual assurance company. I am still [2008] employed as a non-executive director, but that only involves about 20 days work a year.

My long-term intention was to be able to retire early so that I could spend more time enjoying my country pursuits. Having reached 65 I can look back and see the plan has worked. I have been able to fill my time with walking, hunting, fishing, bird watching, gardening and nature conservation work, together with lots of travel to places like New Zealand and Alaska. Long may it continue!

Jill Sharpe, née Jutson (aged 56)

I am in the picture of the class of 1957 [see page 29]. I am the little girl on the end of the second row from the front. I am in a dress with a white collar. I have a photo of me in that dress, which must have been taken on the same day. I was five years old then. I think Sandra Jellyman is also there, the fifth girl along from me, but I am not completely sure.

Also there is Mrs Mabel Legg, the school cook. She

Left to right, back row: *Elaine Jones, Nina Chambers, Maureen Ancliffe, Diane Ancliffe, Mavis Clarke, Lorna Pundsack, Sylvia Waldron, Joyce Lillicrap;* front row: *Linda Walters, Carol Peters, Hazel Damerell, ?, Linda Peters, Margaret Parsons. Jean Vincent, c.1954.*

produced excellent food, along with Mrs Waldron, her assistant. At Christmas they would dress up to give all the children a laugh!

Mabel Legg was 100 years old in 2007 or 2008, living in a nursing home in Plympton. There was a piece in the local paper about her.

She was very much loved by all the children at the school and was always joking and laughing with them. I remember one day she gave me a lift home in her car as I was poorly with a heavy cold. I do not think it would be allowed now but everyone knew her in the three villages. It was very unusual for a woman to drive and own a car then. One of my favourite meals, which she cooked, was meatballs in tomato sauce. They were made of rice and minced beef and my sister Fay still makes them to this day. I also used to love her fish and chips! One thing I did hate was her cabbage, as it contained all the stumps. I could not get these down me so used to drop them on the floor below me if at all possible. You were not allowed to leave anything then!

I used to attend Wotter Methodist Chapel with my great-grandfather, John Selleck, each Sunday, and sit with him in the same pew each week. He was a staunch Methodist. It was his father who founded the original chapel in Wotter at No. 24 Dartmoor Cottages. In later years my Gran lived in the same house. She was the village postmistress and was called Emily May Tucker,

his eldest daughter. The new chapel was built in 1939 and closed after 38 years.

In the picture on page 32 is Mrs Hetty Trethewey, my great-grandfather's sister and mother of Ben, Jean and Christopher Trethewey. Ben used to own the Moorland Hotel at Wotter.

My mother, who is now called Esther Jones, is in the picture of the class of 1937. She is 81 years old now [2006] and still lives at Wotter. She was born in 1925. She was called Esther Tucker then. She is the one holding the cymbals. She thinks this may not have been taken at the school but outside No. 24 Dartmoor Cottages. The boy in the middle is Sidney Phillips. He is holding a triangle.

I think my mother is also in the 1933/34 photograph. She is the child in the middle of the back row with the pinafore on.

Malcolm Clarke (aged 60)

My name is Malcolm Clark and I used to join the Plympton school bus at Collard lane with David Vincent and his sister, Jean.

My auntie, Mabel Legg, was a cook at Shaugh School from about 1956 and still lives [at the time of writing] in St Vincent's nursing home at Plympton. She lived in the Dewerstone Cottage, now the Scouts' adventure centre or similar, in Shaugh Woods from about 1930 till 1956 and will know quite a lot about the origin of the colony. Sadly we have no pictures but I for one was well aware of the hardships faced there, as did many of us at that time.

The Pundsack family lived just across the river in the cottage above the china clay drying sheds, and Brian and Clive went to school with us at Plympton. They soon went to live in Trethewy Gardens, the council houses at Wotter, after they were built in the early 1950s. Roger Parsons became a trade-union leader in Australia, Barry Hawke died of cancer some years ago, David Vincent lives in 2007 at Lower Collard farm with his family. Brian Pundsack joined the RAF and had a bad accident falling out of a vehicle whilst off duty and, despite the large sum of monetary compensation, died about 20 years ago. [Actually Brian didn't die. He rang me in 2007 and we met for lunch at the White Thorn Inn. DB] Romaine Broom married and lives [at the time of writing] in Shaugh opposite the White Thorn public house. My family live in the south of the UK and I married and worked as a teacher for 30 plus years in Plymouth before retiring early from a job which I loved and to which I gave my whole heart and soul Our old head teacher, Mrs Armistead, died in Torquay soon after retirement in the late 1980s.

Susan Lyons, née Walke (aged 57)

My memories of Shaugh School are happy ones, because it was a small school. Mrs Armistead was the head-mistress and Mrs Nelmes was the infants' teacher. She was very religious. Some of my friends were: Wendy Chambers, Linda Peters, Sandra Jellyman, Jill Jutson, Hazel Damerell, Margaret Vanstone, Margaret Parsons, and Sylvia Waldron. We all knew each other quite well. It was quite a long walk to Shaugh each day. [Susan lived on a farm in Goodameavy – DB] I started at Shaugh Prior County Primary School in 1955. Most of the children used to walk to school or come from Wotter on the service bus. I had about 2$^{1}/_{2}$ miles walk to school each day. When I was older mum would stand at the end of the lane and watch us down the hill past Grenoven Farm. Then after a few minutes, she could see us walking up Shaugh Hill. It would not be possible now, as in it is so overgrown. I called for Joyce Lillicrap, until she left to go to Plympton secondary school. We then used to call for Sylvia Waldron and also, some children that used to live in a cottage by the clay works. I think the girl was called Linda Peters. I don't think that they lived there for very long. It became derelict after they left. Pat Faulkner, Justine Balkwill and the Jones family were all going to Shaugh School. Also Mrs Gill used to walk her daughter Petrina with 'Rufy' the dog. Sometimes we used to walk home the back way, as we called it. When I had a birthday party we would all walk home together, all my friends and David Fookes and the Chisholms, who are related to me. I really used to enjoy the school dinners cooked by Mrs Legg. The dinners were really lovely – completely different from today. After dinner Mrs Armistead, the headmistress, would peel an apple.

Susan Lyons (née Walke) and her cousin, Timothy Chisholm, 1957.

The older children took it in turns to have the peelings to eat. She always managed to peel the apple in one long strip. We did PT in the playground and in the summer we did country dancing. At playtime there used to be old tyres to play with and a big skipping rope with two people turning it and all the other children jumping in to skip. We also played hopscotch and rounders. Most of these things would not comply with health and safety these days. When Princess Margaret was married in 1961, the older ones who were leaving Shaugh that year went to the school house to watch the wedding on the TV.

Some days we were allowed to take a favourite toy to school.

Every day we had a third of a pint of milk. If there was no milk available we had milk tablets. The nit nurse used to visit and the school dentist set his chair up in the small classroom. Anybody who was unwell would be allowed to sit by the coke boiler.

Once you moved up into Mrs Armistead's class it was tables and spelling tests. We did our weather and news every day. I can remember on Thursdays after lunch the ice-cream man used to stop outside the school. We could take some money to buy one. On Monday mornings we used to pay our dinner money for the week and also purchase National Savings stamps. Before we left to go to our secondary schools we had to stand up front and recite our times tables, then we were presented with a Bible. I still have mine at home on the bookshelf.

When Pat and I started at Tavistock Comprehensive we stood in the junior hall and felt completely overwhelmed. It took a lot of getting used to, catching the train to school. That was only for the first year because then the railway closed. After that we had to catch the bus. I would love to go back and have a look at Shaugh School to see how much has changed. [Susan did go back on the 8 February 2008. DB] My dad and my grandparents also attended the school. My brother and sister also attended Shaugh. My sister went in 1959, my brother in 1969. There was a new headmaster by that time.

Michael Waldron (aged 65)

I remember most of the kids in the pictures and I remember the Kingwell twins, Jill and Judy, and an incident concerning a pair of trousers down on the moors below their house! Enough said. We did a school play, A Midsummer Night's Dream. I played Puck in it.

Mrs Armistead was head during my time, as was Miss Alford; there was also Mrs Nelmes, for whom I painted a picture of the school on her retirement. I had left school then, of course, and was working for a commercial artist firm in Plymouth after finishing my training at Moorhaven Psych Hospital. The headmaster then was Mr Anstis. Mrs Armistead's husband ran the Moorland Choral Society and some of us sang in it. My mum worked in the school canteen but I cannot remember the name of the cook. [Mrs Mabel Legg –

Left to right: Mr Paxton, Diane Ancliffe, Mrs Trethewey, ?, Mavis Clarke (Titania), Mrs Armistead, Michael Waldron (Puck), John Kennard, Robert Baskerville (Oberon), Mr John Selleck, c.1954.

Scenes from A Midsummer Night's Dream.

DB.] *I do remember lumpy custard, though!!*
There was also a teacher called Miss Hughes before Mrs Nelmes. I had to kiss her when she left (total embarrassment – Miss Hughes was my first crush!!!!). Oh, and the boy who lived on the farm just outside Shaugh was Dennis Baskerville.

A Midsummer Night's Dream

This play was performed by the school in 1954. As you can see, it would appear that the whole school featured in it, quite an achievement for a little school like ours. I've tried to nail down the exact date it was performed but without success, it seems, just like me, all the others who I have contacted and appeared in it are suffering with loss of memory cells. There were a lot of photographs taken and where possible I have provided names, but please forgive me if you were there but your name has been omitted. The following, amongst others, took part: Mike Waldron, Brian Pundsack, Barry Hawke, Eddie Quirke, Roger Parsons, Elaine Jones, Paul Andrews, Paul Harding, John Kennard, Leslie Quirke, Robert Baskerville, Joyce Lillicrap, Mavis Clarke, Diane Ancliffe, David Vincent Malcolm Clarke, Nina Chambers, Maureen Ancliffe, Lorna Pundsack, Jean Vincent, Linda Walters, Hazel Damerell, Margaret Parsons, Leslie Quirke, Paul Andrews, Roger Andrews, Carol Peters and Linda Peters.

Finally

The following poem, strictly speaking, has nothing to do with the Parish, but it tickled me so I decided to include it.

The poem is 'School Days' by Dawn Cawley, a poet from Plymouth and presenter on Plymouth Hospital Radio, and is taken from a booklet of Dawn's poems sold to raise funds for St Luke's Hospice in Plymouth.

I don't want to go to school today
I'm not feeling very well.
I don't want to go to school today
For the children will give me hell.
I know they really hate me
And I'm sure their parents do too,
So I think I'll stay at home today
And spend my time with you.

Now listen to your mother, John,
There's something you should know.
Although you may have problems
You know you have to go.
You'll have to rise above it
And give heed to what I've said.
You've got to face them every day.
Remember – you're the head!

The Craftsmen in the play. Left to right: *Paul Harding, Don Balkwill (Francis Flute), Barry Hawke, Brian Pundsack (Nick Bottom) Paul Andrews, Edgar Quirke, c.1954.*

Taken from an engraving by E. Finden after a picture by W. Westall, published in 1830.

✦ CHAPTER 3 ✦

Shaugh Bridge

Shaugh Bridge is situated on the edge of Dartmoor at the confluence of the rivers Plym and Meavy. In the 'V' formed by the rivers stands the Dewerstone, which is owned by the National Trust. Shaugh Bridge, situated between the villages of Shaugh Prior and Bickleigh, is a beauty spot visited by many people. In the past there has been a small amount of iron ore mining and processing at Shaugh Bridge, and, on the piece of land where the two rivers meet are the remains of a brick and tile manufacturing works adjacent to the remains of an abandoned iron mine. The origins of the iron mine are unknown, but the authority 'to mine and search' for iron was granted to the Ferro-Ceramic Co. in a lease dated 1879. The Shaugh china clay drying works was in operation before the brick and tile works started production. In 1883 the assets of the Dewerstone Iron Mine were put up for auction, because the business seems to have failed. The mine is described on Ordnance Survey maps as being disused in 1886, and the site is depicted as being completely abandoned in 1906. A more in-depth account of the industry at Shaugh appears later in this chapter.

The Bridge

The current bridge was built in 1825 after the old bridge was damaged by a flood in 1823. During that flood it is said that the water level rose by more than 12 feet. The bridge shown below is the old bridge, because if you look at the makeup and shape of the arches you can see they are quite different from later ones. Probably the bridge was quite narrow because in the middle of it appear to be passing places where pedestrians could stand while carts passed by.

The picture on the opposite page was published in 1830 but it is likely that it was drawn prior to that date, so it could very well be of the old bridge. On the bank to the left you can see a house which I believe to be 'Grenofen', (sometimes spelt Grenoven), a mansion originally owned by the Slanning family. In the small booklet on Shaugh Prior produced by the Revd Baring-Gould in 1914, he states that the house was swept away by Sir Massey Lopes, who was the landowner. Whether Baring-Gould meant that Sir Massey had the building pulled down after it was damaged by flood or whether he just had it demolished I cannot verify. However, it would seem logical that it happened after the flood because if the torrent was strong enough to demolish the bridge it is likely that it would also have damaged the property on the river bank.

To the left of the bridge on the Meavy side can still be seen the remains of some sort of building (page 42). We do know from the records available and drawings from that time that Grenofen was built on the river bank, so it would make sense that these ruins are the remains of the mansion.

Drawing of the old bridge, published c.1818.

An 1898 print of a drawing by W.H.Y. Brook.

This line engraving was by M.J. Starling after T. Allom, c.1832. You can tell it is the new bridge, although the house in the back ground on the left seems to be set back further than in the other drawings, possibly due to artistic licence.

The remains of a building by the bridge, possibly Grenofen House.

Joyce Horsley (aged 76)

I, my mother and younger brother and sister lived in Shaugh Bridge every weekend from 1941 to about 1944 during the last war.

We lived near Plymouth Station and our house caught fire in the roof, not enough damage to prevent us living there but as my father was at sea in the Marines, mother took advice from relatives and started moving to Shaugh at the weekends, as that was when the raids seemed heavier. Two relatives and their families already lived in the field at Shaugh full time from Easter to about October. One cousin, a builder, built his family a lovely bungalow complete with a veranda all around it in wood. He told my mother there was an empty shack with a gypsy caravan alongside it empty, and we could rent it, it which we did.

We would catch the train on Friday teatime. At the end of the journey mother would leave me at the station with a suitcase and bags. My two-year-old sister and four-year-old brother would go in the pushchair and be taken down to the field, where my aunt would look after them. Then mother would walk back to the station to get me, aged nine, and the luggage, including bags of food, and back to the field we would go

During the day my aunt would air the bedding so that we had a dry bed to sleep in.

My uncle built his own shack inside the gate to the right. He had a lovely garden in front with veg and flowers. His veg were so big he would have won prizes anywhere. He would never say why his garden was so successful but we do know he made his own manure!

He used to play the accordion and would sit on his front step and play and get all the children singing. My aunt would play the spoons.

As children we had a whale of a time in the woods. Sheep and pigs would roam in the field and woods and the boys used to chase the pigs till the poor things were breathless! We often had to have ticks taken out of legs after playing hide and seek in the tall bracken. These came from the sheep, of course. If we kept very quiet we could watch an old man tickle a trout in the river which runs through the woods. It was fascinating to watch as he'd flick the fish out as quick as lightning onto the bank and we would all clap.

We older children could earn a few pennies by picking berries for a lady who made wine. Blackberries, rowan berries and sloes we collected. We used to collect nuts as well. Beech nuts, head schnapps and edible chestnut. Here the boys would climb the trees and shake the branches and the girls would collect them and share them out afterwards. Wild strawberries grew everywhere and we used to collect them for tea.

Water, as I recall came from a standpipe in the field. There was a water-wheel nearby on the other side of the road with a small shop next to it; here they sold milk, groceries, sweets and, importantly, paraffin, which was used for cooking and lighting.

Shaugh Bridge in the 1930s.

On the rocks at Shaugh, 1907.

Some Saturday nights a crowd of neighbours would climb the hill to the White Thorn Inn. The children would have lemonade and mothers would take sandwiches for the children. Walking home down the hill was very exciting as the bats used to bombard us as we walked and the ladies were afraid they'd land on their heads.

I absolutely loved weekends at Shaugh. We saw all kinds of wildlife – loads of foxes, and the squirrels used to wake us up by running on the roof of the shacks – and birds, especially kingfishers, down by the river. There was always something to see and do. It was heaven being able to sleep at night without hearing sirens go off! We did hear the planes in the distance and by day could see them passing over. Grown-ups would worry about their homes back in Plymouth. The people that had radios would relay the news to everyone. From the top of the hill we could see smoke rising over Plymouth. 'Some poor devil's got hit', someone would say. 'I hope it's not us!'

Going home on Sunday evenings the train used to be full. People used to camp out and put makeshift tents up under trees and hedgerows. From the train you could see these tents and cars hidden under the trees. They'd be like us, just weekend travellers.

To be honest I didn't think anyone would live there

(Shaugh) after the war. Of course I've told my children and grandson all about Shaugh, and they wanted to know why they couldn't spend their weekends there now.

Betty Norton

I lived at Hampool Cottage, between Bickleigh and Shaugh Bridge, from 1933 until 1948 My maiden name was Pullyblank and my father's two brothers farmed at Under Shaugh Farm, now, I believe, renamed Upper Shaugh Farm, in the village, later moving to Bighill Farm off the Plympton road, both belonging to the Maristow estate. There was also a cousin called Tom Pullyblank who was a tenant farmer at Grenoven Farm, Shaugh Bridge. My father, and his sister and brothers, as well as my mother and members of her family, attended Shaugh School. Her maiden name was Phillips.

My memories are very precious to me, as they were happy times and everyone supported each other; rather different from today in many cases.

Brian Willis (aged 72)

I lived at Shaugh Bridge and went to Shaugh School because my parents and I lived with relatives there due to the Plymouth blitz. They were at Shaugh Mill and I was at Endomoor bungalow up the hill opposite the clay dries

From my own recollection the old mill was not used as a mill in my lifetime; the water from the leat was diverted to drive a small waterwheel which drove a generator for electricity. [See the section on the mill later in this chapter – DB.] The old machinery was still there and was mostly of wood but never did anything when we lived there.

The water emptied eventually into the stream that comes down Iron Mine Hill from the village and thence to the Plym. There was once an outdoor privy over that stream at the mill.

Before the war my relatives served teas from a corru-

Endomoor in 2008.

gated addition to the house, and the tea garden remained for some time. The only indoor toilet was in this addition! A Miss Edie Hambly, a family friend, who lived in one of the alms houses at Bickleigh, came over by train to help out and became a fixture.

My 'uncle', actually my father's uncle, Dick Willis, was the farmer and all I remember was that there were a couple of cows and some chickens; not exactly major farming! We used to help bring in the hay, which was always great fun!

I knew Edna and Stan Brown well as they lived close by the mill, and they gave us treats at the kiosk. During the war, the bridge was prepared for mines to blow it up if it ever became necessary, and there was a tunnel just big enough for us children to play in. Also in my distant memory is an old bus that did duty as a venue for the local girls and the men from the radar station at Wotter. In fact one of my cousins married one of them. The bus was located near the kiosk or on Elford's Farm or thereabouts.

When we lived there during the war, I went to Shaugh School and I have fond memories of my mother bringing up jam sandwiches for lunch, and we used to sit by the same stream by the bridge just down from the school.

I had a friend my age, Jeffery Jones [see Chapter 7 – DB], who lived in the little cottage by the loads (clay works) at the bottom of the hill, and we did most of the youthful things that you recounted.

I remember my earliest train trips started at Millbay Station, then Mutley, which then closed. It was a pleasant trip, only a few miles but to a youngster felt like a major expedition and always enjoyable.

I remember the colony and Edna Brown's kiosk just before the bridge.

There was also another 'colony' on the mill land very similar to the one you describe on the way to the station. In fact other relatives lived there also, some year-round; others on weekends, etc. There were three more cabins on the property, all on the lane leading to Lower Meadow. First in Higher Meadow was one belonging to Joe Willis, brother of the tenant farmer at the Mill, Richard Willis. He was away a lot working on the railways in Argentina but he came home and retired there. In the next field was the Mackenzie cabin, whose owners were again related to the Willises at the Mill, and just below them were the Crocombes, more relatives

These cabins were well maintained and lived in. When my cousin was born the McKenzies planted a fir tree! It is still there, I believe.

It was a happy place in spite of the times, and to a small boy it was a great place to be, although one of the Kingwell boys was always picking on me at school! I now [2008] live near Seattle but when we come home on holiday we always endeavour to visit and remember the old places. My cousin whom we stayed with lives in the US also.

I have no idea when the mill was built but it did originally grind because the old millstones were there until the end. There were plans to give it a makeover but I left for the US and when my family who lived there died off, it was sold.

Celia Milne, née Franks (aged 62)

I was born at Bigbury in 1946. My grandfather Pearse had moved the family there as a place of safety to escape the bombing of Plymouth during the war. He was a builder and had built many houses in Peverell.

My memories of Shaugh Bridge are as clear today as if it were yesterday! When we were children my brothers and I would love to climb into grandpa's shining Lancaster, of which he was so very proud. Granny looked so nice in her special Sunday dress, and with great excitement off we would go to the moors.

I will always remember going down the narrow, prim-rose-covered lanes until we arrived at Shaugh Bridge. There was the river with the big boulders, and the sound of the water and laughing children, and we would watch the boys swinging across the river on ropes, wishing we could join in, too.

I was always sent over to purchase the ice-creams from Auntie Edna Kellaway and Uncle Ron in their little kiosk. I remember being fascinated with the array of chocolates, sweets and drinks to buy. It was always such fun. I would stand in the queue with all the other children wondering if Auntie Edna would recognise me, as we had usually returned to Plymouth to see our grandparents and for our holidays, so I had always grown a bit since she last saw me, especially when we came home from three years in South Africa. You guessed! She still recognised me instantly, before I even asked for the ice-creams!

Auntie Edna would always spot me! I think it was my rosy cheeks and pigtails that gave me away! She would say, 'Hello Celia, how lovely to see you. Are you back in Devon and on holiday again? How many ice-creams would you like?'

Auntie Edna Kellaway was my Dad's cousin. They had three children Gordon, Jeffery and Howard.

We attended Auntie Edna's funeral in July 2005. She was buried beside Uncle Ron in Shaugh Church, where they were married and the children were christened. After the service in the lovely little church we all went back to Gordon's house in Plympton. It was great to see him again after so many years, and to meet his family.

The kiosk that Celia refers to was situated on the left-hand corner of the road close to the path that led to the Colony and near Grenoven Farm. The kiosk was originally owned by Stan and Ida Brown, who lived in a bungalow called Somerdale, near Shaugh Mill. The kiosk, which was made of wood, sold all sorts of things – ice-cream, sweets, lemonade, tobacco, ciga-rettes – virtually anything a visitor could wish for. They were open every weekend and most days through the summer. During the winter if they weren't open we could go to their bungalow to buy

things. I remember one occasion when I decided I would try smoking. In those days you could buy cigarettes in paper packets of five. The brands that spring to mind are Woodbines and Domino. I had no idea how much cigarettes cost but I called on Mrs Brown and asked to purchase a packet of Domino for 'My uncle'. Obviously Mrs Brown was suspicious of my demeanour because she proceeded to question me closely about this 'uncle'; how much money had he given me, etc? She quickly saw through my subterfuge and refused to let me buy the cigarettes and sent me away with a flea in my ear. The Browns passed the kiosk on to their daughter, Mrs Edna Kellaway, who Celia talks about in her reminiscences. The kiosk eventually burned down and I later learnt from Jeffery Kellaway the circumstances surrounding this and the reason it was never rebuilt. However, before I tell you, consider this; you may have wondered how ice-creams were kept cold in the kiosk, bearing in mind at that time there was no elec-tricity for the Colony or the kiosk. Mr and Mrs Kellaway got around that by using their freezer at home and freezing ice packs, or ice plates, in it. These were rather like the plastic ice packs we use today in a cooler box, but these were made of stain-less steel, contained water and were the size of a doormat. Every day they would take the plates, together with the frozen ice-cream, down to the kiosk and keep it all in an old refrigerator cabinet. Of course with the constant opening and closing of the cabinet sometimes the plates started to warm up, so one or the other would rush home and pick up another frozen plate and rush back down to the kiosk with it. Eventually Mrs Kellaway sold the kiosk to a man from Southway in Plymouth. Not living close to Shaugh Bridge he couldn't keep replenishing the frozen plates so he decided to install a refrigerator. Now bear in mind that there was no electricity so the refrigerator had to be a gas one. Rather than bore you with explaining how a gas refrigerator works, just accept that you need a flame to create heat to start the process off. Obviously something went

The kiosk was behind this gate.

wrong with it and the result was that the kiosk burned to the ground. An unfortunate accident, but you would think it would not be too much of a major undertaking to rebuild it again, perhaps this time from less flammable materials, like brick or breeze-block. That is where you would be wrong! The Maristow estate who own the land have a rule that if a hut or chalet is destroyed or falls into decay and rots it cannot be replaced by any alternative structure or even one identical to the original. This explains why the chalets in the Colony (see Chapters 4 and 5) disappeared one by one as people left them to move into better accommodation elsewhere.

Justine Elder, née Balkwill (aged 56)

My sister, Justine, was born whilst we lived at Shaugh Bridge in 1951. There was a six-year age gap between us so we didn't really play with each other. Her memories of the same incident are sometimes very different from mine. Many years later she married Shaun Elder, whose family had a holiday chalet at Shaugh Bridge. Although they had known each other as children they lost touch when we moved to Plympton St Maurice. It wasn't until they met again as teenagers that they fell in love and eventually married. They are still married to this day and have two daughters and three grandchildren. These are Justine's memories of living at Shaugh Bridge.

I remember...
... walking alone late at night towards the Colony in the dark from the direction of the Bridge. The path led between the edge of the banked boundary of the Colony and the wood. Feeling afraid, I pretended I had a friend with me who was hiding so anyone hearing would not realise I was alone. I kept calling to my 'friend' saying, 'Stop messing about or we'll be late home and our Dads will be looking for us.' The path was about two miles long (less than 100 yards in grown-up distance). I still think it would be scary there at night.

... Mum blacking the cast-iron stove with a round-headed brush and a tin of boot polish.

... Dad repairing our shoes with an iron gadget like a Manx symbol [a three-footed cobbler's last – see picture in Chapter 6 –DB] using leather or rubber soles and tacks or glue. ()

... swinging across the river with a single knotted rope, usually trying not to get wet but sometimes dangling an arm in the river.

... walking across the parapet of Shaugh Bridge on the Bickleigh side, which seemed wider and flatter, therefore safer!!

... catching the train on Saturday afternoon – some-times missing it and walking on to Bickleigh to catch a bus into town. Mum getting cross with me for walking on all the walls and getting myself untidy and dirty. Mum then spitting on her hankie to wipe off my face and hands before anybody saw me.

... Playing with Jeff Kellaway in a tree which had shoots at its base and which was our imaginary car. We also sometimes played with Timothy Chisholm, who was younger. If Jeff and I were cowboys Tim would be the Indian.

... Learning to ride a bike, realising I couldn't steer and jumping off to avoid hitting a boulder. Riding Dave Fookes's bike – a little blue one which you peddled backwards to stop.

Dave and I once used an old bone we had found as a toy, throwing and bouncing it off a large boulder, it was my turn to catch and it came at me at an angle and hit me in the corner of my eye before I could put a hand to it. I still have the scar and luckily still have my eye.

Another scar which I have is on my right wrist is the result a game we played with the clay lorry weighing machine at the kiln. My hand slipped down the gap at one end and I was lucky not to lose it. The hospital was a long walk and train and bus ride away, so Mum just taped it up, as all mums living at Shaugh would do.

Being a small girl I was often the butt of a joke. Once I was put on the back of the saddleback pig that used to roam the Colony, to see if I could ride it. The pig didn't like it any more than I did.

We liked to run up or across the river on the stones, sometimes playing 'it'. I went home more than once with a wet foot or leg but never fell right in, although I do remember Leonard Ball, who was about my age – seven or eight – falling into a really deep bit and his big sister, Jennifer, looking after him and getting him out. She was only about 10 herself.

We used to race the Royal Marines up to the top of the Dewerstone. We didn't have heavy packs on and they didn't know we were racing them, but we were like little mountain goats and always got there first.

One time I remember being up on a high rock over-looking a sheer drop and my big brother Don, who had

A rope swing across the river.

Justine (with black hair and a papoose back pack) returns for a visit in the early '70s. The little boy with his finger in his mouth is the author's son, Mark, now aged 41.

Shaugh Bridge in 2008 – nothing much has changed.

The front of the Shaugh Mill (top) *and the back* (above) *in 2008.*

Shaugh Mill in the snow of 1978.

more sense than me and no head for heights, crawled across the rock to me on his hands and knees, pleading with me to come away from the edge or Mum would kill him if I fell. [I thought big brothers were supposed to be heroes – DB.]

Our mum had a speech impediment, although I didn't realise it until somebody told me, but I do remember her having difficulties saying 'anemones'. Mum was very clever, very beautiful and always tried to dress smartly. She nearly always wore a hat – not many of the other women did – and although we had very little money she helped other people whenever she could. All our clothes were second hand and came from bazaars (not jumble sales), but Mum still bought and took clothes to a very poor woman who had lots of children; they lived in Mount Gould, I think. I wasn't allowed to tell Dad 'cos he didn't like them, or maybe he just didn't like Mum spending money on them when we were so hard up ourselves. Mum always seemed to look on the bright side and wore rose-tinted glasses, although I sorely tried her patience and sunny disposition.

I never minded school, but I didn't think much of the headmistress (there were only two teachers, one for infants and one for juniors). She always had her favourites and I wasn't one. [I was, because I was a good boy – DB.] I don't remember learning much there but I remember tracing a lion for the front of my geography book. I also remember a school Christmas play where Wendy, Sandra and I were stars. Another time I was an elf searching for buried treasure and confusing a woodsman who had hidden it or was stealing it. I was the elf because I was the only child with an elf costume

at home – we always had lots of dressing up stuff, like brightly coloured scarves, hats and feather boas. Also wigs, gowns and of course a green elf outfit. [A lot of these items had been sent to us by well-off relatives on mother's side – DB.]

During wet weather when we couldn't go out to play, if Don and I were arguing dad would draw a chalk line on the canvas floor covering. Don would have to stay on one side of the room and me on the other. Don used to get the end with the toy box and he used to tease me by playing with the toys and then throwing them at me (at least only the soft ones, I think). Then Dad would get mad again.

There was a three generation family, who lived in the chalet behind ours, who owned a dog, a big fluffy creature – a chow, I believe – and Granny always carried a briefcase with her when she walked the dog. One day we discovered that the briefcase contained toilet paper with which she wiped the dog's bottom. At home we didn't have toilet paper for ourselves – we used cut up squares of newspaper.

My brother Don was very handsome and all the girls liked him and because he was so much older and bigger than me he always looked after me, I was very proud of him and still am. [Notice she says 'was' handsome – DB.]

Shaugh Mill

Not far from the bridge is Shaugh Mill. Nobody is sure of its exact age but it is over 400 years old. The owner in 2008, Joyce Thomas, has lived in the mill

On a return visit to Shaugh Bridge, Tony Foster and the author, aged 17, in 1962.

Another view of the bridge in 2006.

house for over 30 years and has lovingly restored the property from the derelict state it was in when she and her husband bought it. During the war years the house was occupied by a branch of the Willis family and was used as a farmhouse. I can remember calling there in the early '50s collecting' a penny for the guy'. Possibly the family living there then were called Kent because they were the last owners before Joyce Thomas bought it. Whoever it was, I remember that they contributed their pennies. I can't remember the mill actually working, which is hardly surprising since it is supposed to have ceased working as a flour mill in 1922. Elsewhere there is mention of a paper mill being in operation at one time. A 'Heath Robinson' water-wheel did, however, utilise the power of the mill stream in the '30s. A story which appeared in a local paper in 1933 was that Horace Jeffery constructed a water-driven electricity gener-

ator (see page 89) made out of a car wheel, old oil drums, bicycle parts, wood and a dynamo from an omnibus (see Brian Willis's memories page 44). The low-voltage electricity was then run by cable to provide lighting at the cottage attached to the clay works a quarter of a mile away, where he lived with his parents, Fred and Annie (see Chapter 7).

Christine Bryan (aged 56)

Maintaining rural crafts, a ticklish tale...

One bright morning I decided to walk my dog, Meg, by the river downstream of Shaugh Bridge. I rarely met anyone on this side of the bridge, most visitors favouring the tracks leading to the Dewerstone, Cadover Bridge and the Scout Hut. I had often been told that there was salmon in the river and indeed I had seen one or two in the stream which ran through my garden at Shaugh Prior; however I had never seen salmon at Shaugh Bridge. Imagine my surprise, therefore, when, as Meg and I were picking our way across the granite boulders, we came across two beautiful salmon at least 2ft long, not swimming gracefully through the clear waters of the river, but hidden under a boulder. My initial surprise turned to astonishment when I glanced up to see a young man dressed only in a swimming costume, knee deep in cold river water, concentrating hard at something stirring in the river. I had read about 'tickling' salmon, a form of poaching involving many hours standing very still in river water, gently stroking the underbelly of fish until they are transfixed enough to be caught by hand. Clearly, the process was being demonstrated! The young man was initially somewhat alarmed at my appearance, but quickly regained his composure and with a twinkle in his eye looked at me and said, 'Maintaining rural crafts m'dear, maintaining rural crafts.' My response was a stern look of disapproval, together with a mental note to mention the incident to an Environment Agency friend. However, as Meg and I walked away I couldn't resist a wry smile. In this modern age of convenience food, it was good to see that someone was indeed taking rural crafts seriously!

Chris and Bob Bryan now live in a house built on the site of the Brown's bungalow, mentioned earlier in this chapter (see page 45).

Len Webb (aged 62)

In the 1950s our Scout troop was the 1st Shiremoor St Mark's Scout troop and our group scoutmaster was the Revd Donald Maculloch, who had been a vicar in the Plymouth area and had camped in the area before. We travelled from Newcastle upon Tyne by train, changing at Marsh Mills for the line up to Shaugh Prior. At the station we borrowed some luggage trolleys and I think we turned right and went uphill – the total distance was about two miles – before turning into a field near the

The current bridge over the Meavy being manoeuvred into position in 1989.

An early postcard of Grenoven Farm. Note the crossing out of Dewerstone Farm.

village. I do not think it was a regular site; it was a bit bumpy with long grass. One day one of the scouters from Mac's old troop took us to a tunnel... We were taken down a shaft called Drake's Dyke, which was the old water supply for Plymouth. All I can remember is that it was dark, wet and a long way underground. I keep thinking it was by a river but at a greater height. On that day we also went to some man-made pits where you had to balance along the joins. The track we followed went past a very high bank of red soil. The entrance to the tunnel was not easy to find but we went all the way through to the other end. On the way back I found a clay pipe on a ledge. It was quite ornate with a hand holding the bowl. It is a bit confused but it took place in the 1950s. I have spoken to another Scout who was there and he thinks it collapsed in the 1960s. [The location of Drake's Dyke remains unidentified at the time of writing – DB.]

Grenoven in the snow, February 1978.

The footbridge in 2008.

Wooden Bridges

There have been a number of wooden bridges built across either one or the other of the two rivers, the one called the Rustic Bridge was built over the Meavy in 1924. Mr Frederick Jeffery, who lived at the Kiln Cottage, helped in the construction (see p.53).

I believe it was washed away by floods on either 1 or 2 January 1928. In a letter about it in the *Western Morning News* of 11 January 1928, a concerned member of the public who obviously visited the area frequently, describes the bridge being washed away and asks whether anybody would be interested in subscribing a few shillings to have it rebuilt. Obviously no one was, because the bridge was never rebuilt in that location. Another bridge which also

I wonder how long this bridge lasted?

looks quite rustic appears to have been built over the Plym.

A Mr Robert Stribley built a wooden footbridge across the river in the early 1950s when he was the Scoutmaster of the first Crownhill Scout group.

A flood in 1988 weakened this bridge and the National Trust removed it and built their own in July 1989. Where the current bridge stands there are stone supports which are much earlier. These are believed to have been used to support a large pipe across the river.

Margaret Blowey

I attended Shaugh Prior Primary and Tavistock Grammar School. My maiden name was Northmore. My Dad's Northmore family was farming at Goodameavy Barton, near the Dewerstone, for 120 years. This was up the hill from Shaugh Bridge, opposite the way to Shaugh Prior.

I went to Shaugh Prior School for my primary education between 1940 and 1946. I passed my 11 plus at Shaugh. I remember the Colony and a lad called Ronald Ayers, who also attended the school with my two younger sisters and me. Miss Alford was the headmistress at the time and lived with her mother in a cottage just up from the White Thorn Inn. She ended her career as headmistress at Whitchurch Primary School, near Tavistock. The infant children were taught by Miss Skerret. I remember as you went down Shaugh Hill there was a little left turning with a cottage on the left in which a Mr Lillicrap lived. A girl lived there

Rustic bridge c.1925.

The Rustic Bridge on 6 July 1924. The gent in the middle is thought to be Lord Roborough. On the left with the white moustache is Frederick Jeffery, who helped to construct the bridge.

Scouts building a bridge in 1953.

The old pipe supports revealed in 1989. The centre support had been washed away in the floods.

A painting of Shaugh Bridge by Arthur Read of Tavistock.

with hair the colour of carrots, probably his grand-daughter [Ann Lillicrap].

Beside the clay works at Shaugh there was a slagheap where they tipped all the ashes from the fires underneath the clay dries. My sister Mary still carries the scars caused by a coke clinker which rolled down from the pile of waste and caught the calf of her leg. She also used to walk on the parapet of Shaugh Bridge!

I remember a Mr Elford farmed at Grenoven Farm next to crossroads at Shaugh Bridge. A family called Foremost lived in a long bus at the entrance to the farm.

On Lady Day 1946 my father broke the chain and moved from Goodameavy to Peek Hill Farm, which meant I then attended Tavistock Grammar School. We had great fun going to school travelling on the train. The first part of the journey was on the GWR single-carriage no-corridor Princetown train. At Yelverton we changed to join the GWR train going from Plymouth to Tavistock.

I took my scholarship at Plympton Grammar School and passed. At the age of 23 I married a Tavistock farmer and in 2008 we live in a bungalow we built ourselves on our property. Our son John has taken on the farm; the going is pretty hard in agriculture now

Mrs Faulkner with daughter Pat and granddaughter at the bridge, 1978.

Susan Lyons, née Walke (aged 57)

I used to play with Justine Balkwill and visited her home many times. I can remember her mother but not her father so well. I was very friendly with Pat Faulkner who lived at Green Briars. It was to the left of the Balkwill's bungalow; Mrs Faulkner and her son Eddie still live there in 2008. The Joneses lived in the one called Regan and David Fookes and his parents lived at the bottom of the field.

My uncle and aunt were Mr and Mrs Elford, who lived at Grenoven Farm. I lived at Leigh Bere Farm, which was just up the hill from Shaugh Bridge

towards Goodameavy.

Grenoven is now [2008] a private residence and the barns have been converted into living accommodation.

My relations, the Chisholms, lived in a bungalow which was built in the '50s at the top end of the field. Their eldest son was Timothy and his grandparents were the Elfords.

I used to spend many long, happy hours in the summertime at Shaugh Bridge playing, especially with Pat; we used to buy sweets at the shop from Mrs Kellaway and then spent hours jumping the rocks on the river. It was my weekend haunt until I left school and started work in Plymouth as a dental nurse. I have been married for 34 years [in 2007] and live in Bedfordshire. I have three sons. My parents are quite elderly and live at Horrabridge so I visit Devon quite frequently.

Grenoven barns, 2008.

Industrial History

There is no industry at Shaugh Bridge now, but it has not always been that way. Over the years a number of businesses have been set up and operated in the area. All of them eventually closed down. The following article was supplied by Steve Roberts, whose family still live in Shaugh Prior.

The Mining History of Shaugh Bridge and Dewerstone Woods
by Steve Roberts, Plymouth Mineral & Mining Club

Few of the visitors to Shaugh Bridge realise that the car park occupies the site of a china clay drying plant. The large retaining walls of the 'dry' are still apparent, with the settling tanks further up the hill. This might appear to be a strange choice of location for a dry, as the nearest china clay was two miles away at Watts, Blake & Bearne's Wigford Down pit, but it reduced the distance the finished product had to be hauled. The clay flowed from the pits to the dry along a pipeline as a suspension. After drying, the clay blocks were then transported a relatively short distance by road to the railway sidings at Bickleigh.

The conversion from clay dry to car park took place in the 1950s, but several local inhabitants remember working there. A popular walk involves following the course of the pipeline from Cadover Bridge. Much of it is still plainly visible, some sections being ceramic and some cast iron, with occasional inspection hatches along its length.

Ferro-Ceramic Mine and Brickworks. This is situated in the V-shaped confluence of the Rivers Meavy and Plym at Shaugh Bridge. The 6in. OS map of 1904 clearly shows the long parallel walls of the brick kiln and the kite-shaped structures presumed to be settling tanks. It labels two concerns – 'Shaugh Works (disused)' and 'Ferro-Ceramic Mine (disused)'. This would tend to indicate that the two were separate concerns or possibly that the brickworks was not dependent for its raw material solely upon the adjacent mine.

It seems highly likely that iron ore from Shaugh Iron Mine, a deep openwork half a mile away which did not meet the standard required for smelting, may have been utilised by the brickworks after some sort of grinding operation. One school of thought suggests that the occurrence of ochreous clay in this location is unlikely, the country rock being granite, but there are two possibilities; either the material extracted may have been only partially decomposed granite or the site may be occupying a patch of alluvium which could hold all manner of impurities overlying the granite. There is undoubtedly a strong presence of iron, as quite reasonable pieces of brown-red botryoidal haematite may be collected around the site. It could be argued that this would have been

good ore, whereas the soft, weathered material still to be found at Shaugh Iron Mine would have been much more suitable for brick making.

Backing up the theory of material for brick making having come partially from Shaugh Iron Mine is an extract from the *Transactions of the Devonshire Association* 1935:

> *At Shaugh, Mr. Worth led us to the old workings of the iron mines* [presumably Shaugh Iron Mine]. *The ore was in scattered veins and of poor quality, yet good enough for it to be sent away, probably to South Wales. Those were the days of the South Devon Railway, which had at Shaugh Bridge a station for passengers and goods. Such ore which was of too poor a quality to make it worth smelting was used in the manufacture of bricks by the Ferro-Ceramic Pottery Company.*

Furthermore, following his visit to Shaugh Iron Mine on 29 November 1942, Peter Richardson, a well-known local mining historian, made an entry in his records: 'Quantity of yellow ochre lying about'. In a letter he describes how he remembers a gutter near the mouth of the adit to the west of the workings, in which water ran over a thin deposit of very fine-grained yellow uncompacted clay, almost constituting a suspension. It is possible that the ore mined near the brickworks served only as a colouring agent.

Apart from the long, parallel walls of the brick kiln, there are still many traces of the workings. A water-wheel pit may be clearly seen, along with the course of its tailrace heading for the river. The purpose of the stone-lined depression at the western end of the kiln is uncertain, although its position might suggest storage of bricks. The ruinous foundations at the junction of the two rivers were probably offices, whilst the relatively intact stone building just upstream on the Plym side beside the Glenpath was a smithy. The adit opposite the smithy is blocked after a short distance, but its former course is plainly visible from the surface depression. A small tip exists beside the entrance. Just upstream of the brick kiln is another adit, the entrance of which is reinforced by the roots of a large tree. This connected with a shaft, the mouth of which was deliberately blocked some years ago after a bullock fell into it.

Kiln. The two parallel walls of the kiln are still largely intact, the inside faces displaying a rebate of about four inches depth just over a foot up from ground level. Later kilns of this shape moved the bricks through on trolleys such that an almost continuous production could be maintained, but this one would have involved packing, firing and unpacking. This shape enabled a relatively consistent heat to be maintained throughout all the bricks being fired. David Muir has uncovered a patent application for such a kiln.

Water-Wheel Pit. This is in a fairly good state of repair, all walls being largely intact. The approximate dimensions are: length 20ft, width 5ft and depth 7ft max. Presumably, the water supply was via a wooden launder from some way upstream. The course of the tailrace is still plainly discernible, leading to the Plym just before the confluence of the two rivers.

Remains of Small Building. A postcard of 1910 shows the view looking eastwards along the path (described as 'Glenpath') with this building to the right. In the foreground, a man wearing a bowler hat sits on one of the stones that have fallen from the structure. In a 'Then and Now' exercise, with the 'Man in Hat' role played by the Ed, one could not fail to notice that the scene was virtually unchanged after 77 years, the building having deteriorated only slightly. It has been suggested that this was the smithy.

Rubble is thought to be the remains of the site offices. Only the basic outline may be seen, along with a few red bricks protruding through a grassy covering.

Southern Adit. This is open and accessible, with a small tip at the entrance. A collapse after 15ft is reflected in a depression at surface. The reason for the much larger depression on the same line is uncertain – perhaps it was just an open pit, or maybe it was once a shaft that connected with the adit. Fairly rich pieces of haematite are to be found in this area.

Northern Adit. This adit is also open, although after 20ft it is flooded to a depth of about 6ft. It seems highly probable that the adit once connected with the shaft 60ft away. The shaft remained open for many years until a farmer lost an animal in it and pushed the sides in to prevent a recurrence of the incident. Much iron staining is to be seen in the relatively fresh ground exposed.

Stone-Lined Depression. This is now often used for barbecues, but its original purpose is uncertain. The stonework is of a similar type to the other structures on the site. Its position at the end of the kiln suggests a related usage, such as storage of bricks either before or after firing. Perhaps the wells were once higher than today.

Dewerstone Granite Quarries
The assortment of quarries in the Dewerstone Woods area was active mainly in the mid-nineteenth century, all having closed by 1870. Stone was transported by a system of trackways, using standard gauge rails on granite sleepers. The original intention was to connect to the South Devon Railway, which had opened in 1859. The connection was almost completed, with a granite embankment constructed

prior to the final bridge, which would span the Meavy at Goodameavy, but at this point the landowner refused permission to continue and the scheme was abandoned.

Granite was later removed from the embankment and used in the construction of the Lopwell Dam, although much remains.

The two horizontal trackways that skirted the Dewerstone were connected by an inclined tramway utilising two parallel sets of trucks. The added weight of the full trucks on the downward journey pulled the empty trucks to the top in readiness for the next load. To control the rate of descent, a brake house was installed at the top end. In a photograph of 1912 the brake drum is shown to be still intact, but little remains of it today. The brake house itself still stands and the granite sleepers, complete with their bolt holes, are very much in evidence.

The building now known as Dewerstone Cottage is said to have been the former quarry office and smithy. It is now used as a Scout adventure centre.

Dewerstone Rocks are the precipitous outcrops on the eastern side of the hill, overlooking the Plym. Legend says that the Devil rides from the group of stunted, twisted oaks known as Wistman's Wood on certain nights, closely followed by his pack of hounds. Anyone seeing the spectacle feels a strange compulsion to follow to the journey's end at Dewerstone Rocks. Here the Devil pulls up, but the unfortunate follower runs on, to fall to his death!

There are two possible origins of the word 'Dewer'. One is that it is a name for the Devil from the language of the Damoni, one of the ancient tribes of the area. The other is that it has evolved from the name of Tieu, the god after which Tuesday is also named. Supporting the latter theory are old references to Dewerstone Rock as the 'Rock of Tieu'.

The Dewerstone area was frequently visited by the poet N.T. Carrington. The name is engraved on one of the granite boulders at the summit. At one time it was proposed to build a monument to Carrington on the Dewerstone in the form of a small shrine, although this was never realised. His poem 'Lines Written near Shaugh Bridge' begins:

Rude mass, that frownest o'er the downward flood,
how many ages have suffic'd to shake
Thy hoar and fractured crest?

Shaugh Bridge is described as follows by the poet Noel Thomas Carrington:

Oft as noon
Unnoticed faded into eve, my feet
Have lingered near thy bridge, romantic Shau,
While as the sister waters rushed beneath
Tumultuous, haply glanced the setting beam
Upon the crest of Dewerstone.

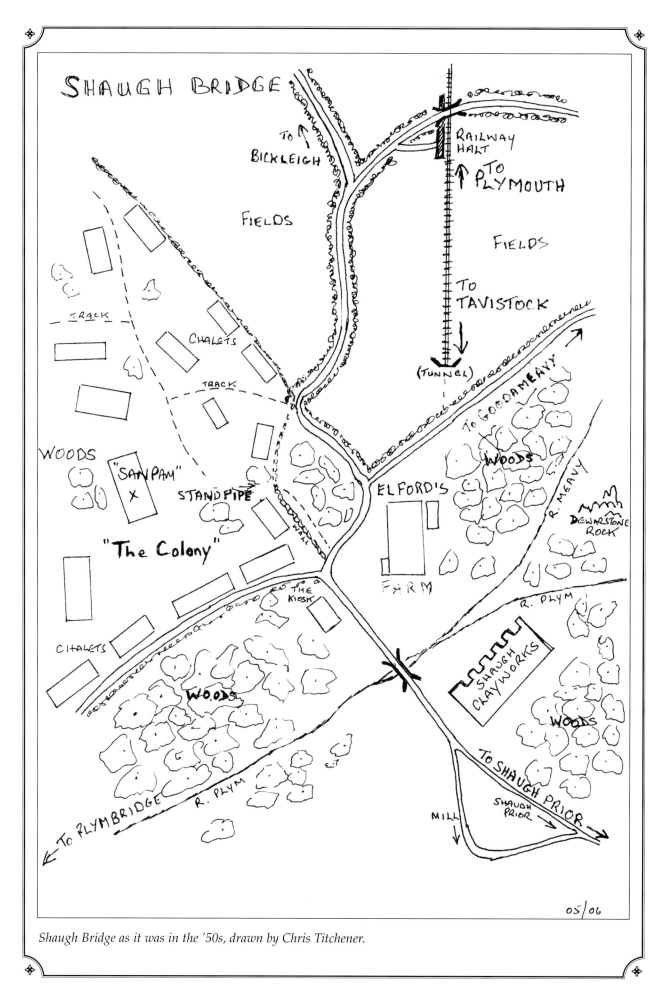

Shaugh Bridge as it was in the '50s, drawn by Chris Titchener.

❖ CHAPTER 4 ❖

The Colony

My mother was left some money, by whom I don't know. With this small inheritance my parents purchased a house in 'The Colony' at Shaugh Bridge. House! It was a shack with a corrugated iron roof. It comprised just two rooms – a living room/kitchen and a bedroom. In my mind's eye the rooms seemed quite large, but remember, I was only a small child, so they probably weren't that big. Of course there is no way of telling now, because the shack was pulled down soon after we moved to Plympton, 11 years later. I should add at this juncture that my sister prefers to call the shack a chalet and my mother always called it a bungalow! So as not to offend my dear sister's sensibilities, from now on I shall also use the term chalet. Our 'chalet' was called 'Sanpam' and it was bought from a couple who had two daughters named Sandra and Pamela, hence the name. They used it as a sort of holiday home. Sanpam was one of about 30 similar but different single-storey chalets in a wooded field called 'the Colony'.

Research into the origins of these chalets suggests that they were built during the Second World War by people eager to escape with their families to the comparative safety of Shaugh Bridge whilst Plymouth was being heavily bombed at night. Plymouth was almost razed to the ground during the war because it was a naval base.

There was no electricity, gas or running water in any of the chalets. Ours was one of about seven that were dotted around a grassy area at the top of the field. Each chalet in the Colony was individual in shape, size and colour and each had its own little garden surrounded by a picket fence or privet hedge. Over the gate leading into our garden was a wire bower, over which mother grew her roses. Our chalet had a wooden frame and the outside walls were covered in flat tin sheeting painted green. The roof was made from corrugated iron and as far as I can remember it was painted periodically with red oxide paint to protect it. The roof was fixed to the beams below with zinc-coated nails about 8cm long. If we had a particularly strong wind or gale, the nails would sometimes work loose and let the rain in. This always seemed to happen at night. We would put buckets and bowls beneath the leaks to catch the water. If it was a particularly

heavy downpour we would need to empty these on a regular basis. When the rain stopped and daylight arrived, Dad would have to climb onto the roof, knock the nails back in and reseal the spot with a rubberised liquid.

Ron Ayers (aged 72)

I suppose I must be five years old. Dark bedroom, curtains closed. Apparently I have got measles. I am wrapped up and carried to Uncle Fred's car, a Ford Prefect. We're going to live in the country and it's a bright sunny day. I don't remember anyone thinking to tell a five-year-old that there was a war on!'

My Dad and his three brothers had a decorating, signwriting and glazing business in Granby Street, Devonport, very close to the Royal Naval Dockyard, which was a prime target for German bombers. The three brothers would go off every day by train from Shaugh Halt to North Road Station, Plymouth, not always sure if the business still existed (in fact, after the blitz No.12 Granby Street did remain, only to succumb to the Council's redevelopment blitz in the late 1950s).

I only know our hut as No. 1, first on the left through the bottom gate to the field. Our neighbours were Mr and Mrs Chidgey at No. 2, and I believe they remained at Shaugh Bridge after the war. The hut backed onto 'the wood' – forbidden territory because I know that my Dad and other men on the site dug holes in amongst the trees to bury the Elsan toilet waste.

Electricity in the hut for lighting and the radio was provided by accumulators which my Uncle Sam charged using a dynamo at Shaugh Mill.

Water, originally, was carried in pails from Mr Elford's farm, but later my Dad and the other men laid a galvanised pipe from a spring issuing from below the railway embankment some 100 yards north of the lane leading to Shaugh Halt. The tap was on the right as one came in the lower gate to the field. At about the same distance but on the west side of the road and dug into

Left to right, back row: *Ron Ayers's dad (Bill Ayers) and two of his three brothers, Fred and Sam – Stan was not present; front row: Ron Ayers, his cousin David (on a visit from Penzance, where he'd been evacuated), David's mum, Ivy, and Ron's mum, Edith.*

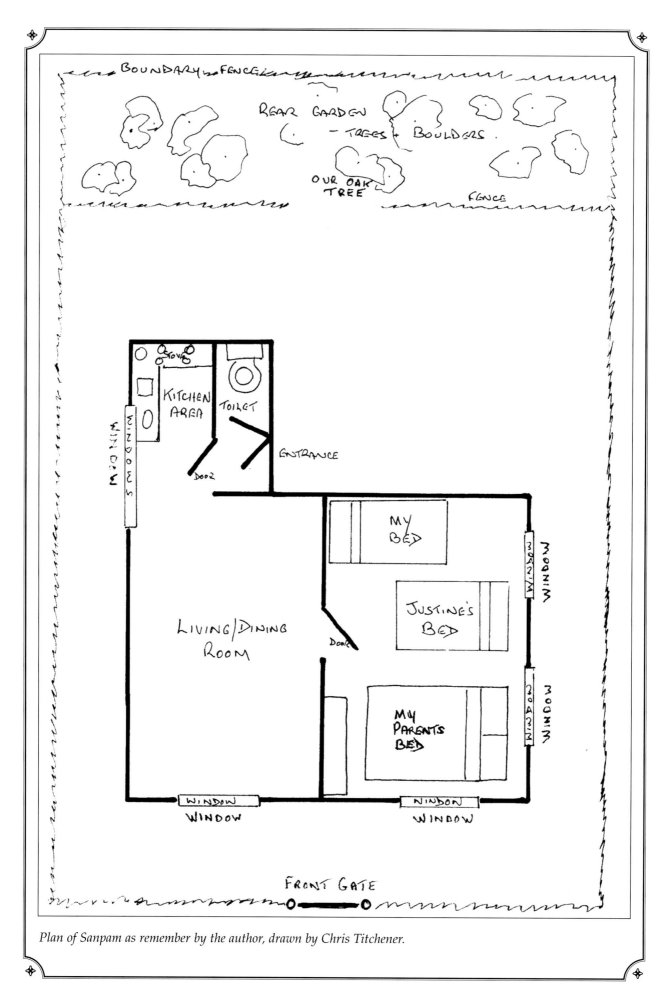

Plan of Sanpam as remember by the author, drawn by Chris Titchener.

Green Briars, where, in 2008, Mrs Faulkner still lives with her son, Eddie.

Norma, Ron Ayers and Jeffery Jones c.1940.

The 15th Battalion Clearbrook Home Guard.

In the years when our Country

was in mortal danger

WILLIAM BLACKWELL AYERS

who served from 29th Sep.1941 to 31st Dec.1944

gave generously of his time and

powers to make himself ready

for her defence by force of arms

and with his life if need be.

George R.I.

Ron Ayer's father's Home Guard certificate.

the railway embankment was an old but inhabited railway carriage which was still there after the war, I think. I also think that on at least one occasion, a long goods train with one Prairie tank loco leading, another in the middle and one banking went up the line, possibly to Yelverton or perhaps to Lydford, where there were government stores sidings during the war.

On the river Meavy (west side) of the Shaugh Bridge itself was a man-made hole in the masonry and I was always told that this was so that the bridge could be blown up if we were invaded. Perhaps someone was pulling my leg.

In the short time we lived at Shaugh Bridge (I never knew it as the Colony) the field containing the huts was just that, a field of grass and bracken, and some tracks leading down river to other dwellings.

I have a picture of the Shaugh years that shows my friend Jeffery, Norma and me. I hate to hurt people's feelings but I'm afraid I do not recall 'Norma'. Mum seems to have been unsure as well but I've seen this picture so often over the years that she seems familiar but I still don't really know who she is. Jeffery, on the other hand, I do remember, as he was really my only friend there. I only knew him as Jeffery Jefferies, assuming, as a five year old, that he lived with his Mum and Dad at the clay works. [In fact this was Jeffery Jones, who lived with his grandparents; see the section on the clay works – DB.]

We would walk up the hill to school every day, usually with one of the mums. On those crisp, dewy mornings, it never seemed to rain going to school and we would poke long stems of grass gently into the spiders' funnel webs then pull back with a squeal when a spider popped out. There was (is) a large flat boulder at Shaugh Prior by the village hall where we would meet our mums for a packed lunch. As we grew older (like six or seven) Jeffery and I would go home unaccompanied, sometimes (despite warnings) across the moor following one of the clay runs to the works. We could smell the clay dries and then his Auntie Win's baking. His home was a wonderful (to a boy) mixture of the smells of the fires, clay drying and baking. I remember once following a clay run on the way home with Jeffery and ended up sliding down a hill of mud, clay and peat. I was not popular that day when I arrived home!

Sometimes we would leave school and the sky would appear almost black with thunderclouds, then almighty claps of thunder and the heavens would open. Funny really, but I have never been afraid of thunder and lightning.

There was a sand pit in the school playground and I seem to remember one of the boys being 'buried' in the sand for a lark! Memories of the class now seem to consist of being happy and doing nothing but drawing Spitfires, Hurricanes and Lysander planes. Sorry, teacher!

I have always regretted losing track of Jeffery after we left Shaugh. My parents told me that he had gone to Cornwall but by then I was back in Plymouth (Stoke) and going to school and I was so sorry to learn that he died so young in 1990.

Dad and Uncle Fred were in the 15th Battalion Clearbrook of the Home Guard and were often out at night 'dealing' with unexploded bombs that Jerry had dumped to gain height quickly on raids on Plymouth. My parents joked later that perhaps Shaugh was not the best place to escape the blitz!

Oblivious, as most kids would be, to my parents' worries I have only the happiest of memories of a time which seemed to last for years and years but was probably only four years. I am not ashamed to admit *that back in Plymouth I would often burst into tears if any sad music came on the radio. I never wanted to leave Shaugh.*

Anyway, the wheel has turned full circle. In 1988 my wife and I bought a two-bed 'box' in three acres of over-grown woodland in South Devon. No railway, no river, no steep hill, no neighbours, no regrets, but still many happy memories of a contented early childhood at Shaugh Bridge.

Fred Winzor (aged 77)

My name is Fred Winzor and I am 77 years old. My birthday is the same as Hitler's. I was born in Plymouth and I was eight years old when the war broke out. Through the war we had a place at Shaugh Bridge. It started out by us going to the Village Hall in Roborough. During one of the raids prior to that we were out one night with another family when an air raid broke out just as we got to Roborough.

We went across the field to a hayrick and spent the night there. We spent quite a few nights in the Village Hall; we used to get a lift out there. One night we had a lift in a furniture van. As we were passing the barracks at Crownhill the gun battery started up and the van was rattling and shaking. All this I remember vividly. Of course this happened several times. Then my brother started driving for a taxi firm and he used to take me out. Then we started going to Bickleigh, where the camp was used for National Fire Service training, and we slept there a few times on straw palliasses on bunk beds in the huts. My father served in the First World War but during the Second World War he worked at Milehouse bus depot. In fact one morning when we went out there there was a bus on the roof. It must have been blown up there by a blast.

When we first went to Shaugh we slept in a little hut which must have been about 8ft square. Anyway, we slept on the floor and then my father started to put some stuff together and in the garden he built the basis of a large hut with a wood frame. The tin walls were made from dried egg tins from the Co-op bakery at Home Park. They were huge tins from America that, split down and pressed out flat, covered the outside. The inside was covered with hardboard. He built a small hut first and then he increased that in size. He even had a water tank on the roof for washing-up water. We had a toilet with a pit for it. No flush!

There were a number of people who lived there that I remember. One person was from London and was responsible for the demolition of the bombed buildings in Plymouth. He used to have a small Morris car and he had petrol so he used to take us into town in that. Most of my time in Shaugh Bridge was spent climbing the Dewerstone, playing down by the river and in the woods, catapults and all that sort of thing.

The people there got together to create and build a community meeting-place. It had a corrugated roof and if the kids were outside they would throw stones on the

roof and it sounded like machine-gun fire. My brother working on the taxis used to get to know people and he got to know this film projectionist and once in a while he would bring out feature films for us to watch. I used to put the records on and that got me interested in the cinema and eventually I ended up running a cinema.

There was a bus down the bottom of the garden next to where the clubhouse was built and there was a family living in it. They had a daughter called Barbara who used to be a pianist in the early days for the silent films. She suffered with arthritis but she was a marvellous pianist; she used to play for parties and that. She had a little daughter called Francis. There was an old-fash-ioned railway carriage just below the railway line where a family lived. They got their water from a fresh water stream that came down from the hill. We always used to stop and talk to them as we walked down from the station. My Mum would go on the train to do her shop-ping. Sometimes my mates and I were up the Dewerstone and we would hear the train whistle in the distance. We would run down the Dewerstone and up to the station just in time to help my mum carry the bags home. That's the sort of life we would lead. We stayed there right through the war. The farmer, Godfrey Elford, had two sons, Peter and Henry; Peter got killed in an accident. They also had a daughter called Esme. It's funny I can remember these names from so long ago yet I can't even remember what happened yesterday. But it was a lovely life, a marvellous life. I still like going to Shaugh Bridge. I spent most of my early life there. I now [2008] live in Plymouth at King's Tamerton.

Rosemary Harrison

I was tickled pink to be sent a cutting from the Western Evening Herald *of 24 May 2006 showing a letter enti-tled 'Shack Dwellers'! I live in London now but the friend who sent me the cutting knew that at one time I lived in Shaugh Bridge with my mother and my brother when he was home on leave from the Army.*

I don't remember the group of dwellings being known

Green Briars in the snow of winter 1978, photographed by Eddie Faulkner.

Mrs Faulkner cosy beside the fire in her chalet, February 2008.

Mrs Faulkner in her kitchen. February 2008.

as the 'Colony', but my mother and I lived in one called *Stepping Stone Cottage* which I think we named. There was a box on the top of the step used as a letterbox. We had no gas, electricity or running water but I think we had the post delivered. How well I remember Aladdin lamps and oil heaters. I don't think we could live like that now.

Unfortunately I cannot recall the names of our neighbours, though we did make friends there. It was my teenage years and I used to travel each day to and from St Dunstan's Abbey from Shaugh Bridge Station. I remember getting on the train out of breath many times, having run up the slope to the station.

David Naylor

Reading about the chalets at Shaugh Bridge awoke memories in my mind of when I was a teenager in the early '50s. I spent some very happy summer holidays there. The parents of a school friend rented a chalet there from a Mrs Clark [Green Briars, lived in at the time of writing by Mrs Faulkner – DB.], who I believe ran the Plymouth cats' and dogs' home, and they would invite me to stay with them sometimes. The chalet was on the left as you entered the Colony and was painted green, as I believe they all were.

I was brought up in a three-room flat in Plymouth with one cold tap and a lavatory down in the backyard, so I was used to roughing it a bit, but that was luxury compared to the Colony. We had no heating, but how they survived all those years there I don't know – must have been made of tough stuff.

As a child I loved wildlife and the time at Shaugh Bridge was heaven as there was so much. We searched

Outside Green Briars, February 2008.

for jackdaws' nests up the Dewerstone and wrens' nest in the stone walls around the Colony. Half a mile downstream we found a deep pool where we would go skinny dipping, a good way to have a bath, and where we could watch the beautiful kingfishers as they would dive into the water to catch small fish. There were always lots of butterflies about in those lovely warm summer days. Another memory is of sloe worms and adders basking on the railway station platform at Shaugh Bridge

I remember the turkey farm below Bickleigh Station. If we found a broody turkey sitting in the hedge, we would poke it away with a stick to get the egg, which was huge and made a great omelette.

All a long time ago when life was very different to now, and when we kids made our own entertainment. No TV or computers in those days!!! But how I wish I could live those times again.

In 2008 there is one remaining chalet in the Colony, all the rest being pulled down as people left the area. It would appear that it was part of the agreement with the Maristow estate, who owned the land, that when any of the huts became vacant or fell into disuse they would be demolished and the land reclaimed by the estate. The remaining chalet is occupied by Mrs Faulkner and her son Eddie, who have lived there for over 50 years. Mrs Faulkner and her family moved into Green Briars whilst we were still living in Sanpam, which was next door. I tried to contact Mrs Faulkner on a number of occasions but without success, then, early in February 2008, I arranged through her daughter Pat that I would call again. It was like stepping back in time and the memories came flooding back.

Mrs Faulkner kindly gave me a cup of tea whilst we recalled old times and people we had known all those years ago. Over the years her children have tried to persuade her to move into premises with all the modern conveniences, but despite not have any mains electricity or gas she prefers to remain where she is. The only 'mod con' they do now have is running water, which is piped from a spring. I returned a couple of evenings later to meet Eddie, and he shared with me his treasure trove of photographs and postcards linked to the area.

I'm very grateful that he allowed me to scan them and they appear throughout this book.

A gate to one of the huts can be seen through the trees.

My first glimpse of the 'lost' Colony.

✤ CHAPTER 5 ✤

The 'Lost' Colony

By now you will know we lived in a field known by some as 'the Colony'. However, there was another group of huts built at about the same time, and for the same reasons as ours, but which was hidden away in the woods. I had heard mention of them but could not remember ever having seen them. Back in May of 2007, when I was still creating the Shaugh website, I had this email from Danielle Fry, who has her own travel website:

Hi Don,
I just had a look at your website and it looks great. I really like the way you write about your personal experiences. My partner, Allen, and I love going to Dartmoor whenever we get the opportunity. Did you know there are a few Second World War bunkers really close to Dewerstone Rock? They were built in case the Nazis ended up coming near there, and you don't know they're there until you're right on top of them. People live in them, but as they're on private land now, they aren't able to do any extensions or too much reconditioning. Once they get too old to live in, they are to be vacated. They're great – no power or water except from the stream nearby. A friend of a friend has one and we were lucky enough to be able to see one of them. It's like living in paradise.

As you can imagine, this piqued my curiosity, so I replied thus:

Hi Danielle
Very interesting story about the bomb shelter. I'd never heard of that before. Any chance of getting a photograph? It would be worth including on the site.

Danielle's reply was:

I've enclosed some pictures of the shelter (see opposite). The woodland picture shows a glimpse of the hut in the background. It's one of the best-kept secrets of Dartmoor, I think, and I feel so lucky to have been there. There are only about four or five there, I think. In one of them a well-known writer or artist used to live. When he died a supposed long-lost relation of his claimed ownership but no one knows if he is really related to him. Pretty interesting... The stream is right next to the hut and on your right as you're looking at the hut from the woodland view the Dewerstone is behind you to the right.

When I saw the photographs I realised what Danielle was talking about. These huts were similar to those that we had lived in. Was there another Colony at Shaugh that I knew nothing about? Were the huts still in existence? My next email to Danielle included the following line: 'What I can't understand is where your huts were and how I never saw them. Can you describe where they are in relation to the clay works, for example?

Danielle replied:

I'm not sure exactly. I remember it's walking distance to Dewerstone Rock. We parked on a road with a parking space for one or two cars, walking through woodland for about five minutes and a decent sized stream is on the right. Behind the hut is a smaller stream. There are about four huts still there. They're in Shaugh Prior. I was speaking to a friend of a friend of ours, who knows you. I don't know his last name but his first name is Andy, and he's recently moved from a house he was living in, in Shaugh Prior. And he knows the huts well. He said that you lived in one of them for 11 years. He has two children, two black Labradors, and is a bit of a hunter-gatherer. I'm sure you know who I mean. [I didn't, but that's another story – DB.]

From the foregoing I couldn't imagine where these huts were, but I was determined to find out because, if the others were as I imagined and they had not been altered to any great degree, then I would be able to show people what the huts were like that we had lived in.

By the end of July I had found someone to take me to them and had made a visit. My wife and I were led through the woods on a little-used track that ran in and out of trees and over little bridges that forded the streams until we came to the first clearing. It was like stepping back in time. These huts were so similar to the ones I knew from my childhood. There were about five of them in a clearing in the woods. Each had its own little garden surrounded by a picket fence or privet hedge. I was later to find there were other similar huts further on in the woods, about a dozen in total. I was lucky enough to be able to chat to a few people who were there at the time. Most are used as weekend or holiday retreats but there is still one that is occupied on a full-time basis. One thing struck me; how small they were. Yet in my mind's eye they seemed so much bigger. I suppose that is because I was a child at the time. All the photographs were taken in 2007/08.

Where are they? I'm sorry but I cannot tell you. Before being shown the chalets I had to promise not

The owner of this chalet stays here on a semi-permanent basis.

What ingenuity! Alex built this hot tub for his children to play in. Water is siphoned from the river into the big plastic canister, a copper pipe takes the water over an open fire and, as the water heats up, it rises and is piped back into the canister. Brilliant!

Photographs of the 'lost' Colony taken by the author.

An idyllic setting.

There are a lot of little streams in the vicinity over which the residents/visitors have built bridges.

These photographs were taken c.1951 and are of the Peters family, Fred and Edith and their two daughters, Carole and Linda. They were visiting Jack Penfold, who lived in one of the chalets for many years.

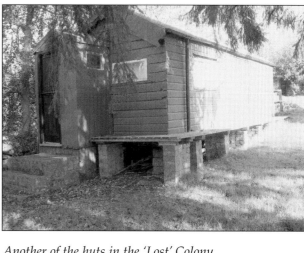

Another of the huts in the 'Lost' Colony.

to advertise the location because the people staying there value their privacy and don't want lots of inquisitive visitors trailing through their hidden retreat. This is a little bit of '30s and '40s history being preserved in its original form, so if you ever stumble across it please bear that in mind.

The 'Lost' Colony? How did it get that name? Well to be honest that's what I called it because it was so similar to what I remembered, and if I were to give you its real name that could give away its location!

Roger and Elaine Smerdon's family had one of the chalets but sadly it burnt down and under the terms of the lease they were not allowed to rebuild it.

This must be pretty chilly on a cold winter's morning!

Above: *Roger and Elaine Smerdon, c.1959.*

Left: *The young sisters, Wendy and Elaine (Smerdon), playing in front of their chalet, c.1950.*

❖ CHAPTER 6 ❖

Living at Shaugh Bridge, 1949–61

The following is an extract from my first book, *Growing up at Shaugh Bridge 1949–61*. It has been included because it was felt that it gives an insight into what my life was like in those times. My apologies to those of you who have read it before:

No Gas. No electricity. No running water. Just think of the difference that makes. We fetched water in white enamel buckets from a stand-pipe that was situated near to the entrance of the Colony, opposite our place. Whether the water came from a spring, a well or a reservoir I don't know, but it must have been quite pure, because we all survived. Many of the things that we take for granted today were not available to us, even if we could have afforded them. Not just lighting and heating, but all the gadgets that are in every household today.

Cooking. All the cooking was done on either the kitchen range, if it was lit, or on a primus stove. I remember we also had a tin oven used for baking. My father had cut a hole in the bottom of the oven which was supported on a shelf. If they wanted to cook something in the oven they would

put a primus stove underneath the hole and that provided the heat in the oven. It actually worked quite well.

In those days pink paraffin oil was the most popular fuel we used in most heating/lighting and cooking appliances

Heating. In the living-room/kitchen we had a cast-iron range, but this was used infrequently. We also had a cast-iron pot-bellied stove and a paraffin heater. We usually used coal, wood or coke for fuel in the range and the pot-bellied stove. Coal was delivered to the Colony by lorry, once a month I think. However, when we were running short of coal my mother, and then later me, would go collecting coke in a sack from the slag heap by the clay works. The coke was created from the coal that was burnt in the kilns under the clay pits. The fires in the kilns must have been very hot because it takes a great deal of heat to turn coal into coke. We weren't allowed on the slag heap so we had to go there when the men weren't working. We didn't normally have any heating in the bedroom, but if it was particularly cold the paraffin heater was brought in from the living-room.

Lighting. For lighting in the living-room we had a Tilley lantern, which hung from a hook on a cross-beam above our heads. It gave out a clear shadow-free light and it also ran on paraffin. However, throughout a long winter evening we had to pump the tank up a couple of times to maintain pressure. You could tell when pressure was falling because the light used to dim. In the bedroom we used a brass-bodied paraffin lamp. All the pictures shown are obviously not the original items, but are very similar to the ones we had.

Washing clothes. Everything had to be washed by hand in a tub and all the water had to be heated in kettles or saucepans. Then there was the drying. The only way to dry any clothing was to pass it through a hand wringer and then hang it out on a line during the summer, and in the winter put it on a clothes horse in front of the fire. All washing-up had to be

Above: *Cast-iron range;* top: *Primus stove;* centre: *Tilley lantern.*

73

To begin with we had a paraffin heater like this.

Brass-bodied paraffin lamp.

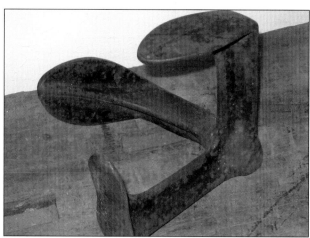

The last, a very clever piece of a cobbler's equipment, provides a secure base whatever way it is used, for large soles, small soles or heels.

Ewbank wooden-bodied floor sweeper.

done by hand and of course the water had to be heated first. As I've already mentioned, the water had to be obtained from a standpipe across the field. I can remember staggering across the field with the aluminium bucket full of water. Mum used large blocks of green soap to do the clothes washing; sometimes she used the same soap for washing us!

Cleaning. Of course there was no vacuum cleaner because there was no electricity, only dustpan and brush. Although I think we also had a Ewbank cleaner that brushed up small items.

Have a look around your house today. How many things can you see that you couldn't use if you didn't have electricity? Refrigerator, washing machine, dishwasher, kettle, microwave, coffee maker, steam iron, curling tongs – the list seems almost endless.

Shoes. My father had a cobbler's last similar to that pictured on which he repaired our shoes. I can remember him tacking a piece of leather or rubber to

Tin baths.

Above: *An old valve radio;* **below:** *an accumulator.*

Wind up Gramophone.

the sole of a shoe and then cutting around the sole to make it fit. He used to buy small sheets of leather and rubber for this purpose. As children we were constantly growing, of course, and I can remember having shoes and boots too big for me so that I would 'grow into them'. Perhaps it was because my shoes were always big that my feet grew to fit into them. I also remember him nailing small half-moon shaped pieces of metal at the rear of the heel of a shoe or boot to slow down wear and tear.

Bathing. We had two tin baths, a small one and a larger one for adults. The water had to be heated on the fire in

kettles and saucepans and everybody took it in turns to use the water. If you were last the water wasn't very hot or very clean!

Entertainment. Although we didn't have a TV, we did have a 1930s HMV wind-up portable gramophone, on which we could play 78rpm records. We had a collection of old records which belonged to my mother. My first ever record was a cover version of Cliff Richard's 'Living Doll', brought out in 1959. We were supposed to change the needle after every play in order to preserve the life of the records, but we didn't know this, so our needles were changed very rarely. I only learnt many years later that needles are available in different 'tones'. Basically, the thicker the needle, the louder the gramophone will play.

An outdoor larder.

We also had various radios. The first one, I remember, was powered by an accumulator, which is something like a small car battery. It was made of clear glass which contained plates of lead oxide suspended in sulphuric acid. Every Saturday my father would take an accumulator with him to Plymouth. There was a shop there that recharged them with electricity. He would take in a depleted accumulator and have it exchanged for a fully charged one. The charge in the battery lasted between one and two weeks, so we always made sure we had a spare available. In the back of the radio were valves that every now and then would blow just like an electric bulb. We just took the back off and plugged in a new one. We used to listen raptly to such programmes as 'Journey into Space', 'The Navy Lark' and 'Children's Hour'. One of my favourites was 'Educating Archie'. The Archie in question was a ventriloquist's dummy. Can you imagine how daft that is? A ventriloquist with his dummy performing on the radio! It's like having a mime artist or a tap dancer performing behind a curtain!

We did eventually have a new radio. We were so proud of it we thought it very posh. This one was powered by a battery similar to the ones we have today but much larger. The brand name was 'Dansette'.

Preserving food. As we had no refrigerator or freezer, all food had to be purchased tinned or fresh, and eaten before it went bad. We had a wire mesh larder where fresh items like meat and milk were kept, but they didn't normally keep for more than a few days. We never had butter, only margarine. I can still remember the brand, 'Echo', and it was horrible! It had a greasy taste that clung to the inside of your mouth. If I had a fishbone stuck in my throat my mother made me eat a knob of it. I still cringe at the thought of it now. Can you imagine how soft and gooey margarine was during a warm summer?

Mealtimes. I've mentioned earlier how poor we were. However, that's not to say we ever went hungry, because we didn't. We always had enough to eat, even if sometimes the cooking went wrong. I did say my Mum wasn't a very good cook, didn't I? My father usually cooked on weekends and he wasn't too bad, even if it was a bit basic. He had worked in the cookhouse in the Marines. I suppose, like most people in those days, we had the same meals on the same days each week, although it did vary sometimes because of the season and availability. Nowadays we eat a lot of chicken because it is freely available and quite cheap. Not so in my day. Chicken was a luxury that was eaten mostly at Christmas. What did we have? Well I suppose it was mainly offal (awful). I can remember having tripe, which you may know is the name given to the lining of the stomachs of various animals. However, most recipes that call for tripe intend you to use beef stomach lining. Tripe is almost always sold bleached and partially cooked. This saves a lot of work, since unprocessed tripe would need to be cooked for many, many hours to make it tender enough to chew. I'm sure the thought of tripe has made your mouth water.

Another 'delicacy' was chitterlings, which are the intestines of a pig, so there are miles of it. They are boiled or fried or both. I can just imagine you smacking your lips at the thought of them. Sorry to disappoint you but you won't see them for sale very often in this country anymore. I think we always bought them ready cooked. In their raw state they were, and still are, used as sausage skins.

We also had liver, which I never liked because it was always hard. It was only years later that I realised it was Mum's cooking that made it that way. I love liver now, provided it's cooked very quickly and is still bloody.

Another unusual dish I remember having was cow's udder, which, as you should know, is where the milk is stored on the cow. It looked like a joint of very pale beef and had a very unusual texture. Another big piece of meat which we sometimes had was ox or beef heart. That also had an unusual texture. It can be sliced like beef and is dark red in colour. You can still buy lamb's hearts but I haven't seen beef heart for years.

Sometimes we had home-made pasties. They were always bigger than the ones you could buy in the shops and I seem to remember that our pastry was always heavier. We also had commercially made pasties. When I went to Plymouth with Dad we frequently called into a place called Selleck's, where they sold pies and pasties. However, we didn't go into the shop at the front, we went around to the bakery at the back and bought them direct from the baker himself. Now whether they were day-old pasties, or the baker had a little sideline selling them for himself, I don't know, but I do know we didn't pay the shop price. I also remember they were very tasty.

Pasties originated in Cornwall and were first made by the tin and copper miners' wives. Tradition has it that the original pasties contained meat and vegetables in one end and jam or fruit in the other end, in order to give the hard-working men 'two courses'. Today there is still debate about exactly how a genuine pasty should be made. Many will tell you that a pasty can only be made with short pastry, while others will advocate puff pastry. However, the issue that invites the most controversy involves the famous 'crimp', the wavy seam that holds the whole pasty together. Should the pasty be sealed across the top, or at the side? History suggests that the crimp should be formed at the side, because the pasty has always been eaten by hand, and the side crimp is the most convenient way of holding onto your lunch while you take a big bite. As it was originally intended as a miner's meal the crimp would probably have been thrown away because it was dirty. Bear in mind the miners couldn't wash their hands underground. There are some facts that can be agreed upon by all pasty-makers. The meat should be chopped, the vegetables should always be sliced, and the ingredients must never be cooked before they are wrapped in the pastry. Each pasty must be baked completely from raw.

One of Mum's favourite meals was herring, a cheap and nutritious fish, and kippers, which are smoked herring. However, the trouble with herring is the number of bones in them. I seem to remember we also had quite a lot of tinned pilchards and sardines. I suppose this is what started my lifelong love of all things fishy. I still eat sardines regularly, but I prefer them skinned and boned. The tins are also much easier to open today because they are the ring-pull variety. When I was a boy each sardine can had its own key, rather like the key you get on a tin of corned beef today, only longer. You would insert the little tongue of metal on the can into the key and then wind the lid around the key. At least that is how it was supposed to work. Sometimes the tongue of metal snapped and you had to cut open the can with a tin opener. Did I say cut? I should have said rip! The earliest opener I can remember us using literally tore open the can and tore the fish as well. Later we progressed to the butterfly tin-opener. That type is still in use today.

Another fishy thing my Mum loved was cod roe. This delicacy falls into two categories; hard roe and soft roe. Hard roe is in a sac or bag containing hundreds of thousands of fish eggs found in the stomach of a female cod. Eating it is very peculiar because each mouthful is like eating thousands of grains of edible sand. Each egg is no larger than a pin head. On the other hand, soft roe (also called white roe) is found in the male fish. Milt, as it is also called, has a totally different consistency, being quite smooth in texture. Mum used to prefer hard roe whilst I preferred soft roe, and I still do. We used to have it fried on toast. You are unlikely to see it for sale in a supermarket these days, but it can often be obtained from an independent fishmonger, or you can buy it tinned.

During the week we usually had cereal or porridge for breakfast. The porridge was always thick and glutinous with brown sugar sprinkled over it. For some reason we only had brown sugar in our house. My mother believed it was healthier. On the weekend it was different. We had faggots for breakfast on Saturday and fishcakes for breakfast on Sunday. Both were fried. Another treat on Sunday was a cup of coffee, only it wasn't coffee as we know it today. It was 'Camp' coffee, which came out of a bottle as a thick, black, syrupy liquid made from a mixture of coffee, chicory, sugar and water. It was made in Scotland and is still available today.

Before we went to bed I always had a cup of Bourneville cocoa and Justine always had Bournvita. One thing mum was good at was making chocolate sweets from porridge oats and cocoa. We loved them.

We had milk delivered by Ernie Edwards, the milkman. It sometimes went off before we had drunk it because we had no refrigerator. As I've already mentioned, we only had a wooden larder with wire mesh to let the air circulate but keep the flies off the contents. Ernie also delivered eggs. I know the price of them in 1951 because my mother wrote it down on the back of the note she left for him when Justine was born. In 1951 six eggs cost 2s.6d., roughly 11p in today's money.

Bread was also delivered. Every week a baker's delivery van would come to the Colony loaded with bread and cakes. It would be a real treat to climb into the back of the van and choose a fancy cake as a special treat. I think the bakers were called Goodbody's.

Childhood ailments. Like all children I had the usual childhood ailments, including coughs, colds, chicken pox and measles, but I never had to go to hospital for any ailments. I had the usual scrapes and bruises that most children have, but luckily no broken bones. I did have weak ankles and consequently had quite a few strains and I also seemed to get laryngitis quite a lot. Mum's remedy for all these was the same. Iodine! I can remember her painting my throat with yellow iodine and making me wear an old strip of cloth pinned around my neck, and that was for a sprained ankle! No, I'm only joking. It was for laryngitis. I hated it. The iodine didn't wash off for what seemed like weeks, so even when I was better my neck was still yellow. It came in a little brown bottle with a dropper in it.

The other thing my mother swore by was cod liver oil! It's horrible, but it has been proved that she, along with all the other mums of that time, was right to give their children that horrendous-tasting liquid, because recent research has shown it is beneficial. Another medicine of the time which tasted awful was castor oil, which was used to ease constipation or as an emetic to induce vomiting. It is notorious for its strong taste.

Shaugh Bridge was a beautiful place to live and I had a wonderful time exploring, rock climbing and building dens. Nowadays, to get across to the piece of land between the rivers there is a wooden bridge spanning the River Plym. When we lived there you had to jump from rock to rock to cross the river, or walk on a rope strung across whilst holding on to another rope strung above.

The ropes were installed by the Royal Marine Commandos, because they used the area for training during the '50s. There was a third method, a rope swing. That was great fun. The bough to which the rope was tied stretched out over the river. We could take off from a tree on one side of the river and land on the other river bank. There was a knack to swinging across the river without getting wet. Imagine a rope with a knot at the end of it being like the round bit at the end of a pendulum. When a pendulum is vertical that's when the round bit is closest to the base. When the rope was vertical the knot at the end was very close to the water. To avoid going into the water as we swung across, we would put ourselves into a horizontal position with the rope across our stomachs. We became very adept at using the swing rope, sometimes doing tricks like swinging upside down and swinging from tree to tree. We would perform these tricks when the 'townies' came to visit the area at the weekends, and used to encourage the visitors to have a go themselves. This was not because we were being particularly helpful – it was to serve our own purposes. When they had all gone home we would wade through the river picking up the coins that had fallen out of their pockets when they were swinging upside down! This mostly happened in the summer, and then it only yielded a few coins. The local farmer, Mr Elford, removed the rope on a number of occasions, but it was just replaced with another. This went on for a number of years, like a game, us putting up a rope and farmer

Elford cutting it down. Finally Mr Elford solved the problem, as he saw it, by sawing down the tree from which the rope was hung. Game, set and match!

Although we were quite poor when I was a child, because Dad was out of work for a long time, I can't ever remember feeling deprived, that is until I went to grammar school. I had very little in the way of pocket money. However, I was able to earn some extra money for myself. One of the ways of earning a few extra pennies was to collect pop bottles. In those days there were no plastic bottles, they were all glass. Visitors would come to Shaugh for the day and buy bottles of Corona pop from a little shop called the kiosk, where first Mrs Brown and then her daughter, Mrs Kellaway, used to sell sweets, tobacco, cigarettes, crisps, other odds and ends and, of course, pop. The kiosk was situated on the road close to the path leading to the Colony. In those days the pop bottles were recycled, but not as they are today. The lemonade company wanted their bottles back so they could be used over and over again. To encourage people to return their bottles they would charge a deposit of 3d. on each bottle when the lemonade was bought. The 3d. would be refunded when you brought the bottle back (3d. was roughly the equivalent of 1p today). Some visitors stayed until the early evening, by which time the kiosk was closed, so instead of taking the bottles home with them they just threw them away. That was OK by me because we would collect them up and, the next time the kiosk was open, return them and claim the deposit.

I also used to collect jam jars to take to a farm in Bickleigh Vale. The farmer kept bees and was happy to receive as many jars as I could supply, which, unfortunately, wasn't that many. He would pay for them with broken honeycombs dripping with honey. I would chew the wax comb to extract every drop of honey. Delicious! I would watch him using a smoke blower on the hives to calm the bees down. He would then lift out shelves, which were about 12cm square, in which the bees has created honeycombs of beeswax which were full of honey. They were a work of art in themselves. He never wore a hood or protection, yet I never saw him get stung. He used to leave jars of honey on a ledge outside his farm gate so that passers-by could purchase the honey. He had a sign on them which said 'Take the honey, leave the money'.

Don't run away with the idea that any of these activities produced substantial amounts of money, because they didn't. The amounts were very small and intermittent, but any extra money to spend on myself was appreciated. Having said that, my parents did buy us treats. Every week my father would go to Plymouth to get the weekly shop. Whilst there he would buy two bags of sweets of differing varieties. Every evening my sister and I were allowed to choose two sweets each. I suppose this did us no harm, because both of us still have our own teeth.

I also earned extra pocket money by working on the farms around about. The milkman, Ernie Edwards, had his own farm, which in truth was very run down. However, I worked there on a few occasions, haymaking. A number of children and I would follow behind his tractor, picking up the hay or corn. At dinner time he gave us a home-made pasty each, and we sat in the field eating it. It could have been a scene which Constable would have painted. Sometimes, at Christmas, I helped him plucking chickens. I remember that Mrs Edwards had a very large dish in which she had thick clotted Devonshire cream settling. Lovely!

Ernie was quite a character. The name of his farm was Mount Clogg. I suspect he was always struggling to make ends meet, because his farmyard was littered with broken down and rusting machinery. He mostly delivered his milk in a van, which was constantly breaking down. I remember more than once, along with other children, pushing his van to try and get it started. He would put it into gear and then a great cloud of smoke would erupt from the exhaust and off he would go again. The van was lopsided because the suspension was gone on the passenger side. If you sat in the passenger seat you were pressed up against the door. If the van wasn't working he would do his deliveries on a motorcycle with the milk in the attached sidecar. Even the motorcycle was a wreck! In those days there were no electric starters on motorbikes. You got it going by turning the engine over with a foot pedal. It's called a kick start. The pedal was held on with a piece of wire. Like all farmers, Ernie had a tank on the farm which held the fuel for his tractor and other machinery. He always left it to the last minute to have it refilled. I remember clearly, on one occasion, when it was right down to the dregs of the tank, the fuel had to be filtered before being put in the tractor because it was brown with flecks of rust from the inside of the tank. I said he was struggling to make ends meet. Perhaps it wasn't that, perhaps he was just mean and didn't like spending money. After all, as they say, 'you don't see a farmer on a bike'.

At times I also worked on Mr Elford's farm mucking out the cowshed and helping him in the fields. However, that wasn't that frequent because he was very slow in paying, and tried to avoid paying all that was due. I can remember helping to cut logs on a large circular bandsaw, which was belt driven from the tractor. There was no guard on the saw and I could have easily sliced a hand or even an arm off. But I guess they didn't worry as much about the safety aspects as we do today. It was great fun riding on the back of his tractor when we went cutting kale. Kale is a green-leafed plant which was used for feeding cattle. If you took the hard outer cover off the stalk, you could eat the pith. It tasted rather like fresh garden peas.

Once I had a little job where I was paid peanuts Literally! It happened this way. As already mentioned, there was the kiosk run by Mrs Kellaway. Well behind where we lived there was another chalet occupied by a Mrs Gill, her young daughter and her mother. Mrs Gill had a bit of a reputation as a scarlet woman. Perhaps it was because she was the only young women in the Colony without a man. I don't know whether it was justified or not. Anyway, Mrs Gill decided to set up her own little shop in competition to the kiosk. She had a shed attached to her chalet that had originally been an outside toilet. She had shelves fitted, painted the inside of the shop and stocked up with all sorts of confectionery and general groceries. What a Public Health Inspector would have said about this I dread to think! Every weekend when the weather was fine, Mrs Gill paid me to go to the next little hamlet of Bickleigh and then on to Bickleigh Bridge in my little trolley. Bickleigh Bridge was also a beauty spot and very popular with visitors.

I would go down by the river to a grassy open space where the visitors were and sell crisps, nuts and chocolates to whoever wanted them. Later in the day I would return to Mrs Gill with the unsold items and give her the cash for what I had sold. She would then pay me a commission, not in money, but in sweets or usually in packets of KP peanuts, because I loved them best of all. I hope you are not thinking 'pay peanuts and you get monkeys' is very apt!!! Mrs Gill's foray into commerce didn't last very long and she had to close down. You could say that all her aspirations were flushed down the toilet. Although in Mrs Gill's situation that wasn't true because there was no running water!

Another interesting pastime was scavenging for food that the Royal Marines had left behind when they were on exercise at Shaugh. A few miles down the road was Bickleigh camp, home of 42 Commando and a training school for the Royal Marines throughout the '50s. Frequently during this time we would have troops of marines carrying out exercises all over the area and staying one or two nights under canvas. They used to carry all their food with them and most of it was tinned. They had things like Irish stew, corned beef, vegetables, steamed puddings, condensed milk, biscuits, margarine, jam and sweets. The marines, having completed their exercise and eaten all they wanted, would then bury all the cans, including the unopened ones, to save having to carry them back to camp. When they had gone we would hunt out the spots where things were buried and dig them up to take home. Sometimes the cans had no description on them, so it was interesting opening them to find out what was inside. My favourite was a golden syrup sponge pudding, although the tins of sweets were also very good, too.

I suppose collecting up all these tins, bottles and jam jars could be called my contribution towards

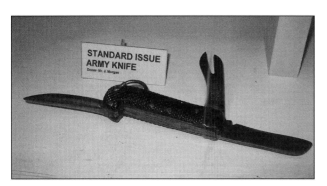

A jack-knife.

keeping the countryside tidy and an early form of recycling. However, to be honest I never thought of it in those terms.

Immediately after a Royal Marine exercise there were always things to be found that had been lost or left behind. I had a collection of solid fuel stoves, billy cans and literally dozens of folding tin-openers. A couple of times I found a jackknife which all Marines seemed to carry at that time. They were great, they had a blade, a tin-opener and a spike which I assume was to get stones out of horses' hooves. Funny; never used that tool.

I was always finding used blank cartridges and occasionally live ones, too. I used to open the live ones, pour out the explosive and try to make fireworks. They were not very successful and created more smoke than explosion. Thinking back on it I was very lucky not to injure myself, or others for that matter.

I once found a Lee Enfield .303 rifle hidden behind some rocks. This was the weapon that the Marines were equipped with at that time. Presumably it had been left there by a deserter some years previously because the wood on it was starting to rot. I handed that over to a group of Marines on exercise.

On one occasion I actually took part in a night exercise. Somehow I got talking to the officer who was in charge of the exercise and he asked me if I knew of a suitable spot that they could use for their HQ during the exercise. I told them about, and showed them, the house beside the china clay works, which had been vacated by the Peters family and was now derelict (see Chapter 7). This proved to be ideal for their requirements. I can't remember whether I asked, or whether it was suggested that I took part in the night exercise. Whichever it was, the officer came with me to see my parents and obtained their permission for me to participate. Thankfully they agreed. When I say I took part I don't mean that I ran around all night firing a gun. No such luck. Rather I stayed with the officer and the HQ unit crouched down in the lee of the bridge and listened to the progress of the battle over the radios. I did get to fire a flare pistol to start and stop the exercise. I was probably

around 12 years old at the time and it was all very exciting for a lad. Unfortunately I never went on another exercise with the Marines, although I did try to persuade other troop commanders to let me take part, but to no avail.

Besides playing in the woods and climbing the rocks we also played and swam in the River Meavy. In the early years, the Plym was too polluted with clay to swim in, so I learnt in the Meavy. That was Dad's doing. We would be walking along the riverbank and he would push me in to teach me to swim. That wasn't so bad, it was getting out of the sack that was the real problem. Joke! There weren't many pools in the river that were suitable for swimming. However, there was one that was reasonably large which was downstream from Shaugh Bridge towards Bickleigh. We spent many happy hours there. The pool was situated at a spot where the river ran past a meadow; the Scouts used it as a campsite. Even now, when I have difficulty in sleeping, I can close my eyes and visualise myself lying in that grassy meadow on a warm summer's day, the sun high in the sky and the sound of the river in the background. It is very relaxing. Both my Dad and I tried to teach Justine to swim, but we didn't have much success. On one occasion, when I had taken Justine to the pool, I decided I would use scare tactics to get her to swim. I went out to the middle of the river and started thrashing around. I shouted for help, pretending I was in difficulties. Justine just ignored me and carried on playing on the beach with the sand and pebbles. So much for that idea! We visited the pool when we returned 50 years later. There was a father watching his three children playing in the water. It made me wonder just how many children had played at that spot before I was born. How many had played there since? How many more will play there long after I am gone? I wonder what I'll wonder next?

We also used to play 'Pooh Sticks' on the river, although it didn't have that name when we played it. To play the game you throw sticks off a bridge into the water, then cross to the other side of the bridge to see whose stick comes out first. The game features in A.A. Milne's book *Winnie the Pooh*.

I also used to go fishing in the River Meavy, even though we weren't supposed to (there were no fish in the Plym because of pollution.) I used to go up the river towards Meavy until I found a secluded spot. I never really caught very much. I can remember one occasion catching a very small trout which really should have been thrown back, but I was so proud of it I took it home. By the time it had been cleaned, the head and tail removed, and cooked there were no more that a few mouthfuls left to eat, but I enjoyed every morsel. On another occasion I caught a freshwater eel and took that home. Freshwater eels are very difficult to kill. They bite and are usually quite small, about 30cm long. Similarly, by the time it had been prepared and cooked there was hardly anything to eat, and it made such a mess of the pan. Whenever I caught one after that I never bothered to take it home because it really was not worth the effort. I used to catch minnows and take them home in a jar, but they died within a few days no matter how many times I changed the water.

Sometimes we made bows and arrows and used to go hunting for rabbits. Not that we ever caught any, because the arrows didn't have any flights, so they didn't fly straight. The bows didn't last very long either, because they were usually made from hazel branches and the wood had not been seasoned. Not that it mattered, because the fun of it lay in making the bows and arrows, finding a field with rabbits in it, and trying to creep up close to them so they didn't hear us, but they always did. We also made catapults from V-shaped sticks, and tied strips of rubber to them, cut from the inner tubes from car or cycle tyres. If the weather was bad and we had to stay in, we sometimes read a book or got out our dressing-up box and played 'make believe'. We had a box which contained cardboard milk-bottle tops, strips of raffia and lengths of wool. Where this came from, or why we had it, I don't know. It's very strange when you consider that cardboard milk-bottle tops were discontinued in the 1930s and we were playing with them in the early 1950s. The tops were about 4cm in diameter and you could push out the centre. From these we used to make pom-poms. I would explain how, but it's too difficult without having the items with which to demonstrate.

Christmas. I don't remember much about Christmas at Shaugh Bridge. Only one really stands out. That was when I received a very large cardboard box filled with comics. My mother had bought them at a jumble sale. I can't remember specifically which

comics they were but I do remember that I was able to follow the serial stories, because the comics were all in sequence. They were probably a selection of the *Eagle*, the *Lion*, the *Tiger*, the *Dandy* and the *Beano*, all of which were very popular in the 1950s. That was a magical Christmas because I loved reading, as I still do. My love of reading I inherited from my father, although our tastes differed. He loved space stories and westerns, where my tastes veer toward tense thrillers and autobiographies. When Dad went to Plymouth every weekend, he took the books he had read to the pannier market and swapped them for replacements at a second-hand book stall. If I went with him I would take my comics and do the same. Dad carried on taking his books to town and swapping them right up to the time he became incapacitated.

Anyway, to get back to Christmas, we never had a Christmas stocking, but we always hung up a pillow-case at the end of our beds. I know it can be difficult today sneaking into a child's bedroom without waking them. Imagine what it must have been like for my Mum and Dad; after all, we all slept in one room. We always had a Christmas tree, although it wasn't exactly the traditional Christmas tree, which is the Norway spruce. We went and cut down a tree in the local forestry behind the railway station. I believe they were Scots pine and therefore were more spiky and didn't have as many branches as a traditional tree. However, it is the thought that counts.

We also decorated the living-room. This was usually with garlands and paper chains like we made at school. On Christmas eve or the closest day to Christmas day when the market in Plymouth was open, Dad went to town and waited until just before the butchers' stalls were closing, to try and get a duck, chicken or perhaps a goose at a reduced price.

A picture of the clay works from a newspaper dated 5 February 1939.

The clay drying in a kiln.

✦ CHAPTER 7 ✦

The Clay Works and Jeffery Jones

When we moved to Shaugh the only industry in the area was farming and the china clay drying pits. Throughout the year, but particularly in winter, the River Plym was very often like a river of milk flowing from Cadover Bridge because of all the clay that had escaped into it. The liquid containing the clay was piped from Cadover. Due to its extremely fine nature (finer than silt), clay was mixed with water and transported through pipes to Shaugh as a liquid slurry. It was then stored in huge square stone vats which had fires below them, evaporating the water and leaving solid blocks of china clay. Lorries then took this solid china clay away. We weren't supposed to go into the works where the slurry pools were, but I can remember going on the walkways between the vats when the workmen had gone home. If I had fallen in I would never have survived.

I have put the clay works together with the details on Jeffery Jones because so much of what is here was supplied by the descendants of Jeffery. They live in Canada. One of the pleasures of creating the website was that I could put people in touch, sometimes with long-lost friends, and sometimes, as in this case, with people who knew their father as a boy. In this instance it was Margaret Blowey, Ron Ayers and Brian Willis, who all knew Jeffery as a child.

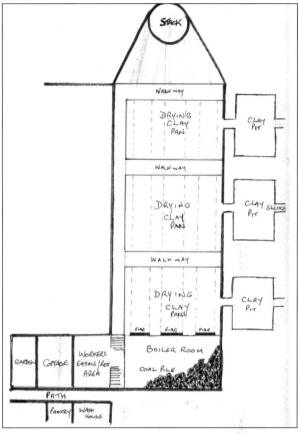

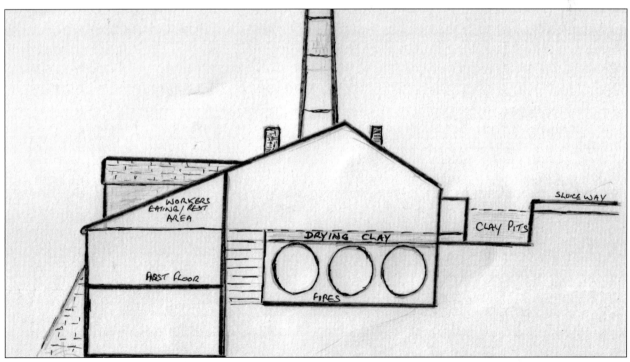

Above and top right: *Drawings of the workings of the clay works made by Jeffery and redrawn by Chris Titchener.*

83

Notes from Jeffery Edward Jones, who was raised by his grandparents, Fred and Annie, and lived in the cottage from 1935 to 1944

My earliest memories centre around the tiny stone-built cottage, built as part of a china clay works drying kiln, which was constructed in 1888 at Shaugh Bridge. We were there because my granddad, a real jack of all trades (carpenter, blacksmith, haircutter, cobbler and saw sharpener) had worked as a maintenance man for the clay company. He and Gran were married in 1900 and I believe moved straight into the cottage – they certainly had their six children in it (William, Elsie May, Frederick, Hilda, Horace and Winifred). Quite an achievement considering it had precisely two small upstairs rooms and two slightly larger ones downstairs – no running water, walls that oozed dampness, little light and must have been as unhealthy as one could get. I don't recall it ever getting hot, although there was a total lack of fresh air – particularly in the back bedroom –1 a long, narrow room with a tiny window at one end. The cottage was built into the clay works in such a way that the back and one side were completely blanked off – the back wall was, in effect, the vertical rockface of the

Jeffery in front of the cottage in 1936.

bank, while the side wall was the end wall of the drying kiln shed. We also had a small workers' eating place (filthy with coal dust from the kiln boiler room) immediately above the back bedroom.

It seemed normal – probably because as a child I was so isolated that I saw the insides of very few other houses, all primitive, but some fairly large farms and other tiny cottages – all stone built.

While I don't remember great heat, the cottage certainly got cold (probably emphasised by the permanent dampness) and it was normal to sleep with tomorrow's clothes in the bed. Occasionally a kerosene heater was used to warm up the parlor and/or the front bedroom.

The house had been wired for low-voltage electric light run from a small water-wheel-operated generator half a mile away at 'The Mill' – a small farm serviced by a millstream originally for a large mill-wheel but later for a much smaller water-wheel.

The Jeffery History

Frederick Jeffery married Mary Ann (Annie) Ash in 1900 at St Jude's Church in Plymouth. By 1901 Frederick and Annie were living at Shaugh Bridge. Frederick was 27 and worked as a clay miner. They lived in the small cottage attached to the clay works.

The stone cottage was built in 1888. There was a front room, a kitchen/dining room in the back and two bedrooms upstairs. The back wall of the cottage was built into the side of the rock face.

Frederick and Annie had six children in 12 years, three boys and three girls. William John was born in July 1901, Elsie May in May 1903, Fred in January 1906, Hilda Annie in September 1908, Horace George in June 1910 and Winifred (Win) Marjorie in September 1913. In December 1915, at the age of 14, William died in an accident at the nearby mill.

The children attended Shaugh Prior Primary School. Win worked as a school teacher at Shaugh Prior until her wedding to Spencer Prideaux in 1937.

Frederick was a handyman/carpenter and we were told he was involved in the building of the bridge. He built things out of wood for inside the church and had the 'first running toilet' in the area. He also played the violin. Annie used to run a tea shop at Shaugh Bridge which was used by day trippers from Plymouth and area.

Fred junr married Lillian (Bill) in 1928. She was previously married to a white tea planter in India. Hilda married Frank Jones in 1929. Frederick and Annie's first and only grandson, Jeffery Edward Jones, was born on 12 July 1935 in Exeter. Frederick and Annie raised Jeff in the cottage at Shaugh with the help of his aunts and uncles.

Fred and Horace, his sons, built the small water-wheel mechanism used to generate power (see the article about the mill in Chapter 3).

Fred junr bought a garage in the Ridgeway,

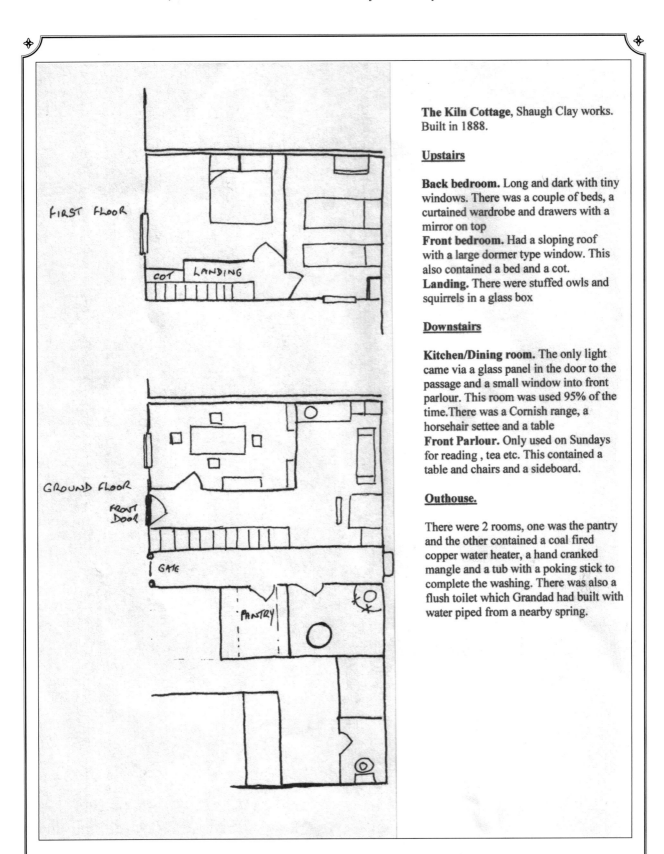

Jeffery's sketch of the interior of the cottage, redrawn by Chris Titchener.

The Kiln Cottage, Shaugh Clay works.
Built in 1888.

Upstairs

Back bedroom. Long and dark with tiny windows. There was a couple of beds, a curtained wardrobe and drawers with a mirror on top
Front bedroom. Had a sloping roof with a large dormer type window. This also contained a bed and a cot.
Landing. There were stuffed owls and squirrels in a glass box

Downstairs

Kitchen/Dining room. The only light came via a glass panel in the door to the passage and a small window into front parlour. This room was used 95% of the time. There was a Cornish range, a horsehair settee and a table
Front Parlour. Only used on Sundays for reading , tea etc. This contained a table and chairs and a sideboard.

Outhouse.

There were 2 rooms, one was the pantry and the other contained a coal fired copper water heater, a hand cranked mangle and a tub with a poking stick to complete the washing. There was also a flush toilet which Grandad had built with water piped from a nearby spring.

Fred and Annie Jeffery, 1900.

Fred and Annie Jeffery outside the cottage in 1936.

Plympton, during the 1930s known as the Ridgeway Garage. Horace joined Fred at the garage after the Second World War. They moved to larger premises at St Mary's Bridge, Plympton, about 1955. This garage was known as Jeffery Bros. They remained there until their retirement in 1972/73.

Frederick died in 1944 at the age of 70. The family continued to live in the cottage at Shaugh Bridge until 1946. After attending Shaugh Prior School, Jeff

attended Plympton Grammar School in 1947 and Plymouth Grammar School.

Annie died on 29 October 1947. Jeff was raised by his Auntie Win and Uncle Spence (Prideaux) in Cornwall after Annie died.

Jeff grew up with his aunt and uncle in Falmouth. Win and Spence owned a butcher's shop on Arwenack Street and lived above the shop. After living at the shop Win and Spence opened a guest-house in Falmouth. They later moved to St Agnes.

Jeff was a good student and went to London University to study physics. He met Vivienne Jones through his good friends from Falmouth while at university in London. They married on 16 May 1959.

Jeff and Viv had three children in England and during that time (1960s) they moved around quite a bit through Jeff's work with nuclear power plants. In 1968 they moved to Canada and they had another child in 1969. Jeff worked with Ontario Hydro, the provincial power utility, to begin with, then, in 1975, he took a job in management with NB Power in New Brunswick. There he worked his way up to be Director of Technical Services of all the power plants in the province, including a large nuclear power plant. He was incredibly respected and liked by all – people to this day speak of his kind, warm and generous spirit.

Jeff was a huge history buff, and read non-stop. He loved Canada. The family visited England quite regularly over the years, as all the family still lived overseas.

Jeff died in 1990. Before he died he wrote the notes about his life as a child at Shaugh Bridge and included sketches of the cottage as he remembered it. He told us many stories of his life at Shaugh.

Jeff's ashes are buried at Shaugh Prior at his grandparent's grave. His middle name, Edward, was after the church at Shaugh Prior.

Ros May (aged 45) and Sue Robinson (aged 38), daughters of Jeffery Jones

I know Dad loved living at Shaugh and had a wonderful family who raised him. In fact, when he died in 1990 my mum and his Auntie Win buried his ashes at the church at Shaugh Prior with his grandparents. Win died in 1996 and is also buried there. Dad was in fact named Jeffery Edward Jones – Edward after the church. I believe his grandfather was involved with some of the woodworking inside the church.

Our dad would have lived in the cottage before that. He was born in 1935 and we know he lived there through the war.

He would have moved (we think) sometime around 1945 (maybe a bit before). He had a granny and a grandfather and their children were William, Elsie May, Hilda, Fred, Horace, Winifred (there may be one more). Our father's mother was Hilda. She became ill during his birth so he lived in the cottage with his grandparents and some of his aunts and uncles.

They all somehow fitted in this cottage by the clay works – our great-grandfather was the handyman or something or other at the clay works (he also had some other jobs). Our father, before his death (he died in 1990), wrote some notes down about his childhood (he was forever telling stories about Shaugh). Our Auntie Win (the teacher Winifred Jefferies) also kept a journal every day of her life

There is another drawing dad made of the interior of the cottage – what furniture they had, etc. It certainly shows the living conditions at the cottage.

It looks like Fred and Annie met in Tavistock, were married in 1900 in Plymouth (her home) and were living at Shaugh Bridge in the 1901 census. Fred died in 1944. Annie died three years later. Both are buried at Shaugh Prior. Our father lived in the cottage from 1935 until 1946. We have photos of him at Shaugh Bridge in 1946 still taken in front of the cottage at the works. We know his grandfather died in 1944 so assume the family was allowed to stay there for a few years. We are not sure of this but have quite a

Fred and Annie Jeffery, 1939.

few photos dated after Fred's death. There is a photo of dad's class – Form 1c, Plympton Grammar School – dated 1947, and by 1950 he attended Falmouth Grammar School and was living with his Auntie Win.

Fred and Horace opened a garage in Plympton, Plymouth. We remember being there as children but are not sure which place. Horace died a few years ago but his daughter Sandra still lives in Plympton. After her marriage Win moved to Falmouth, where they had a butcher's shop. They later moved to St Agnes, Cornwall.

Fred and Horace, on top of building that water-wheel mechanism [see page 75] we believe also built the first working toilet in the area. I could be wrong, but for some reason think Dad mentioned that to us! And we believe they did not have to go to war, because they recharged batteries, did mechanics, etc., during the war locally. That would explain why they opened the garage in Plympton. It was still there in

Left: Jeff and May Jeffery, October 1944.

The wedding of Miss Winifred Jeffery on 2 October 1937 at Shaugh. Win taught at Shaugh school in the 1930s. In the back row, fourth from left: Winifred Lillicrap, who lived at Spring Cottage, just up the hill from the clay works; middle row: ?, ?, ?, Spencer Prideaux (the groom), Annie Jeffery, Frederick Jeffery; front row: Horace Jeffery, May Jeffery, Jeffery Jones, Winifred Prideaux (Jeffery), Frederick Jeffery junr.

Jeffery with Form 1c at Plympton Grammar School in 1947. He is in the back row to the left of the very tall lad.

Photo: Hornbrook.

HARNESSING THE PLYM.—Mr. H. Jeffery, of Shaugh Bridge, has constructed a water-wheel from an old motor-car wheel, the louvres being fashioned from old oil drums. Bicycle chains and wheels, together with a dynamo originally used in an omnibus, complete a successful generating plant.

Newspaper article dated 3 November 1933.

the mid-1980s – with the old-fashioned pumps. Fred's wife went by the name of Bessie – she was older and, from what I remember hearing, was an eccentric American. I think she started up a baseball league in the area. This would have been in the late '30s or early '40s sometime. That probably was in Plympton or Plymouth though. Dad was a child at that time.

We do know that Dad lived with his auntie (Elsie) May and Annie (grandmother) after Fred died (just with the two women). We are not sure where exactly

that was. We think all the other children had left by that point. We always thought it was somewhere else (other than the cottage) – but could be wrong. For some reason we don't think Annie died in the cottage. If she died in 1947 and Dad was at Plympton Grammar School that year – maybe they (Annie, May and Dad) had moved into Plympton.

I have lots of 'stories' in my head but only visited Shaugh when I was two so some of it doesn't make sense to me.

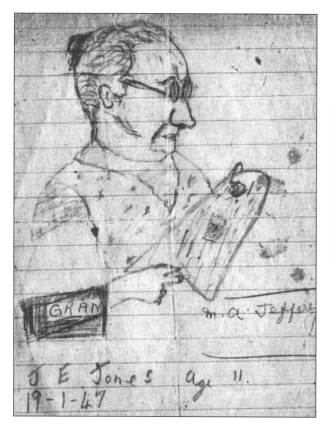

A drawing of Annie (Gran) made by Jeffery when he was 11 years old.

Winifred and Jeffery, 1937.

I was young, nine or ten. We also had picnics with them. I know Horace and May had a daughter; Fred and Mrs Jeffery did not have any children

Mum used to do Fred and Mrs Jeffery's housework and some cooking at their bungalow in Wotter. I used to go sometimes in the school holidays. I would play in Wotter and have lunch with them .

I think it must be Mum in the photo of Win and Spencer's wedding; don't know where Dad was!

The Pundsacks

After the Jefferys the cottage was occupied by the Pundsack family. As I recall they had quite a few children themselves. There were Anthony, Mervyn, (twins) Una, Brian, Lorna and Clive. They all lived in that two-bedroomed cottage. They moved to a house

I think Dad said he played in/at the mill with his friends in the evenings and played in the woods, as well as hiding underneath a platform (at the station?). My mother said he had a set of twins that he played with (boy and girl, I think) when he was young in Shaugh. I think he may have been in the choir.

Mostly he told stories of his childhood during the war and what they had to eat, etc.

Joyce Butcher, née Lillicrap (aged 61)

My Dad and Mum were great friends with Horace and Fred Jeffery, I expect because they lived in the kiln cottage and we lived just up the hill at Spring Cottage.

I remember Mum and Dad talking about Win Jeffery, and my sister remembers Jeffery Jones.

Fred and Horace had the garage at St Mary's Bridge, Plympton. Dad bought his first car from them, and always went there for repairs, etc. In fact I think he bought all the cars he ever had from them.

I knew both brothers; Horace and May lived at Plympton and Fred and his wife (can't remember her first name, I always called her Mrs Jeffery) lived at the top of Collard Lane, Wotter. Mrs Jeffery was very involved with the Red Cross (she had lived in India). She is in the photo of a Christmas party at Wotter Chapel hall sat in the front beside the vicar (page 129). I remember she took me to the ballet in Plymouth when

The clay works, c.1920/30.

Carol and Linda Peters outside the cottage, c.1953.

The site of the clay works is now used as a car park by visitors.

Mark Twain and said 'The rumours of my death have been greatly exaggerated'. We have met and talked a number of times since then, so I can testify that he is alive and kicking.

The Peters

After the Pundsacks came the Peters, Fred and Edith, with their two daughters Carol and Linda. They had lived in a tiny caravan near the mill. Fred worked at the clay pits at Wotter; you will see a photograph of Fred in Chapter 11 sitting on a dumper truck with a German prisoner of war standing in front of it. There are also photographs of the family in Chapter 5. Fred continued to work at Wotter but also became a sort of night watchman at the Shaugh clay dries, keeping the fires stoked overnight. Although there were only two rooms downstairs Edith turned the front room into a tea room, serving cream teas and refreshments to the weekend visitors. She also made toffee apples, and Linda tells me that she and her sister had to loiter around the bridge with toffee apples in their hands in the hope that visitors would ask where they got them and they could direct them to their mother's tea room. Linda also tells me they were under strict instructions not to eat the toffee apples but to take them home for reuse.

The Peters family moved out and went to live in Plymouth in about 1956, when the clay works at Shaugh closed down. The cottage was left empty for a while and it was at this time it was used as HQ for a Royal Marine night exercise. I tell the story of that occasion in Chapter 6. The works were then demolished and the area is now used as a car park for the many visitors who come to the area.

in Trethewey Gardens in Wotter around 1950. They were a very nice family and I can recall visiting them with my mother in Wotter. I was friends with Brian in particular because we were the same age. Both of us passed the 11+ and went on to grammar school, Brian to Plympton and myself to Tavistock. After leaving school we both joined the Royal Air Force. We met only once during that time. Years later I heard that Brian had been very seriously injured in a road accident. Years after that I heard that he had died as a result of these long-term injuries and I know some of our contemporaries heard the same. Imagine my surprise when I picked up the telephone to hear a very gravelly voice say: 'Hello Don, this is Brian Pundsack'. He could quite easily have quoted

Shaugh Halt, c.1907. The tunnel can be seen in the distance, which is no longer possible because the embankment is now covered in trees and bushes.

CHAPTER 8

Shaugh Halt

When we lived at Shaugh Bridge the closest bus stop was at Shaugh Prior, where I went to school. The only other public transport at Shaugh Bridge was the train that travelled from Plymouth to Launceston and back. This stopped at Shaugh Bridge Halt, which was about a 5–10 minute walk from the Colony, where we lived. The railway line was opened on 22 June 1859. Shaugh Halt opened in 1907. The line was nationalised as part of British Railways in 1948.

Passenger services were withdrawn on 31 December 1962. Freight services ceased and the line closed completely in 1964, three years after we had left the area. Our leaving had nothing to do with it. The trains themselves were steam trains, pulling a variety of carriages. Most of them were the type that had compartments that seated about eight people, with a corridor running the length of the carriage, giving access to the compartments. At either end of the corridor there was usually a toilet. The other common types were the ones with individual compartments but no corridor, which meant that, between stations, you couldn't change compartments or go to the toilet! If you were desperate you just had to cross your legs. Mind you, it wasn't unknown, if the carriage contained just schoolboys travelling to or from school, for the windows to be opened. I leave the rest to your imagination. Hope nobody further back had their windows open. The last carriage on the train was usually the guard's van, which was used for large pieces of luggage and parcels.

There is a tunnel almost immediately as you pull out of Shaugh going towards Tavistock. I walked through it a few times when the trains

The tunnel today – a walking and cycling track.

The waiting-room, c.1962.

were still using the track, but not at the same time as a train was going through, I hasten to add. I wasn't that brave! Or stupid. Even though the line is now closed you can still walk through the tunnel because the track has been turned into a cycle and walking route from Marsh Mills to Clearbrook. The tunnel itself is curved, so when you get to the middle you can't see either end. When I last walked through the tunnel you needed a torch, because if you didn't have one you were in pitch darkness when you got to the middle. You couldn't even see a hand in front of your face. However, since that time there have been safety lights installed through the tunnel.

There is a video available which shows the very last passenger journey made on the line on 29 December 1962. If you are interested it is available from Archive Films, based in Hooe, Plymouth. They also have a variety of videos of old train journeys.

Shaugh Bridge Station
Compiled by Graham Eagle
from many different sources

The South Devon and Tavistock Railway Co. (SDTR) made a successful bid to build the railway in 1854, the bid being supported by the then Earl of Morley. The line was opened on 21 June 1859. Isambard Kingdom Brunel was engaged during the construction of the line to succeed the deceased presiding engineer. Viaducts along the line were timbers on granite piers, but these were replaced by stone structures between 1893 and 1910. The line was extended to Lydford and Launceston in 1865. The Great Western Railway (GWR) Co. absorbed the SDTR in 1878. It was converted from broad to standard gauge in 1892. It was closed as uneconomic in 1962 as part of the 'Beeching Cuts', the last official day being 29 December of that year. The track was lifted in 1964.

The length of line between Bickleigh and

The station in the 1950s.

A train arriving from Plymouth.

The station in the 1950s.

A train coming in from direction of Tavistock some time before 1960.

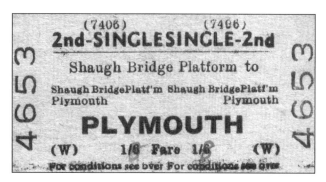

Top and above: *A second class single to Plymouth on 3 May 61 cost 1s.6d., roughly 5½p.*

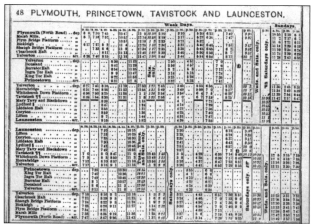

A Plymouth to Launceston railway timetable, pre-1956 because it includes the line to Princetown, which closed in that year.

An early postcard marked 'Shaugh Bridge Halt'. However, the shed in the background looks nothing like the waiting-room at Shaugh.

Clearbrook is the one of particular interest to this history, so this section is described below in more detail and traces a journey along the line, travelling north.

● The gate at Bickleigh opens upon the old Bickleigh Coal Yard.
● Ham Green Viaduct. The original piers of Brunel's wooden viaduct can be seen besides the present valley crossing. The granite replacement was built in 1899. The viaduct is 190 yards (174m) long and 91ft (28m) high,
● Ham Green plantation
● Hele Lane Bridge
● Shaugh Platform. Here was a siding for loading iron ore from the NO EMIE Mine at Shaugh Bridge. Initially there was no provision for passengers and this aspect was not opened until 19 August 1907.
● Grenoven Wood. Just before the line enters the southern end of the tunnel, a tubular iron aqueduct can be seen crossing the line on stone piers. This was erected in the mid-nineteenth century and serves a leat carrying water from Hoo Meavy weir to Wheal Lopes.
● The tunnel (known locally to the Scouts as 'Smokies') is 308 yards (282m) long and bends slightly so that one cannot see one end from the other. About two-thirds of the distance through the tunnel, there is an adit branching off to the right. This was first called Bickleigh Vale Phoenix and later Tunnel

Mine. It comes to a dead end some 50 yards into the hillside
● A short walk after reaching the end of the tunnel you will notice a leat crossing under the track. This is the same Wheal Lopes leat we saw in the aqueduct at the other end. It too navigates through a tunnel, which should not be entered without proper safety precautions.
● Goodameavy Bridge is the next landmark, where the road from Goodameavy Manor goes under the line and up 'Market Hill' towards Roborough Down.
● The line continues then to Clearbrook Halt, which operated between 1828 and 1962. This part of the line is not open right through because the land at the Clearbrook end is privately owned. However, a path has been created up the hill to reach the village opposite the Millennium hall

The railway track is now a cycle route from Laira in Plymouth to Clearbrook, and forms part of National Cycle Route 27.

CHAPTER 9

The Dewerstone

On the land made by the V where the two rivers meet is the Dewerstone, which is a large hill or tor. The term 'tor' is most commonly used in the South West of England, particularly with reference to the high points of Dartmoor in Devon and Bodmin Moor in Cornwall. At the top is the Dewerstone Rock and the Devil's Face or Rocks. To get to the summit you can either follow the old miners' track which zigzags its way to the top, or you can scramble and climb your way, following one of the numerous tracks that have developed over the years. When I was a child I thought the Dewerstone was the name of the huge rock at the very top. Having done some research on the subject it would appear that the whole area, including the cliffs and rocks to the right of the summit, are also called the Dewerstone Rocks. However, on their own these are called the Devil's Rocks. There are three distinct pillars which, for climbers, range from easy to very difficult. The highest is said to be around 150ft tall. The Royal

Justine and Shaun Elder enjoy a picnic with their two daughters, Tracey and Sarah, in the woods at the base of the Dewerstone in the 1980s.

Painting of the Dewerstone by Henry Wimbush, published as a postcard between 1904 and 1908 in the 'Oilette' series.

This is a postcard from 1910 showing the start of the walk up the Dewerstone. The postcard is mentioned by Steve Roberts in his piece on the industrial history of Shaugh Bridge on page 57 'remains of a small building', thought to have been a smithy.

Shaugh Bridge, Glenpath, Plymouth

Marines used them for training in rock climbing. They are also used by civilian climbers. They can be quite dangerous and a number of people over the years have fallen to their deaths from them. When I was young we used to clamber up the rocks without any climbing gear at all, although we never climbed the sheer faces. One of my most shocking memories is of a Royal Marine falling from the rocks and injuring himself very badly. I must have been in my early teens at the time. I was near the Bridge straddling the rivers when they brought him back from the rocks. He was being carried on stretcher and he was moaning, 'Oh my God! Oh my God!'. I asked if there was anything I could do to help and one of the Marines suggested I went back to the base of the cliff from which he had fallen and collect his boots, which they had taken off. I went back along the River Plym to the spot where they had been climbing and found the boots. By this time it was dusk and as I reached down and picked up the boots they felt quite sticky. I looked closely at them and to my horror found they were covered in blood. I don't know what thoughts were going through my mind as I ran back. I only know I was very, very scared. We did learn a few days later that the climber had died.

Whether it was a result of that experience, or just getting older and wiser, I don't know, but there was an occasion when my sister Justine and I walked up the Dewerstone using the normal route, which was steep but not dangerous. I must have been in my early teens at the time. When we got to the top we walked over to the Devil's Rocks. Justine walked to the very edge of the cliff and was peering over. I, on the other hand, would not, and stayed over 2ft from the edge. Justine, being six years younger, had not yet learnt to fear danger and still had the impetuosity of youth. Justine remembers me saying: 'Come back from the edge, Justine! If you fall mum will kill me!'

Legends

The first occasion I was told the legend of Dewer nearly frightened me out of my life. I don't remember how it came about, but I had to walk back from Wotter on my own, just as it was getting dark. I must have been about nine years old at the time. Brian Pundsack, who was the same age as me and a bit of a lad, told me the story before I left to walk back home. It was the Dartmoor legend of Dewar the huntsman, also called the horned man, and his pack of fearsome, ghostly dogs known as the Whist Hounds. The legend goes that when a storm rages across the moors the Wild Huntsman is riding again. Some say he hungers for human blood, or for the souls of unbaptised babies. Dewer would also drive unwary travellers to their deaths over the highest cliff on the Dewerstone: the 150ft high Devil's Rock. To catch sight of his terrible hounds would cause you to sicken and die within the year. The hounds are

white, enormous, and have eyes and ears the colour of flame. In other versions of the legend, the huntsman is the ghost of Sir Francis Drake. Although Drake became a hero, he started off as a pirate and had a reputation for being very cruel. Another story goes that a farmer riding home from the Warren Inn, an ale-house high on the moor, once saw a hunter with a strange pack of dogs, glowing eerily in the mist. Drawing on all his courage, he asked the man if he'd had good sport that day. The hunter laughed and threw the farmer a bundle, making a gift of the kill. The farmer shuddered and hurried home, the stranger's gift under his arm. When he reached his door he unwrapped the bundle, and found his own child, dead! As you can imagine, after hearing Brian's version of this story I was terrified walking home on my own in the dark and started to cry. I had walked about a mile when I saw a figure coming towards me. I didn't know whether to run or hide. Luckily for me the figure shouted out. It was Mr Pundsack walking home from Shaugh. He could see how distressed I was and walked me almost the whole way home.

A walk up the Dewerstone
supplied by John Partridge
Classic walks on Dartmoor
http://www.btinternet.com/~jhpart/v1cycleh.htm

Shaugh to Dewerstone.
½ hr. Easy stroll.
Start point Shaugh Bridge. Grid Ref 534 636.
Shaugh Bridge is a local beauty spot on the south west of the moor to the south of Burrator reservoir.

There is a small car park and bus stop beside the bridge at the bottom of the hill at Shaugh Prior.

From the car park beside the long hill leading up to Shaugh Prior, there is an old large granite set of walls for the main car park. [*The old clay works – DB.*] From the car park, walk away from the road, north-west to the wooden bridge, which is hidden from the car park just upstream of the road bridge.

The road bridge, mentioned as 'ponta de Cada worth' in 1281, was damaged and replaced with the present bridge in 1823.

The name of the River Plym, or Plymma, is from the Celtic word 'pilim', 'to roll'.

Further upstream, on Dartmoor, the Plym was also known as the River Cad, a Celtic word for skirmish, at Cadover Bridge.

Route to the top of the Dewerstone
Over the wooden bridge, follow the path to the right to take the old cobbled quarry track up the hill. If you look closely on the left-hand side just before the start of the path you will see the entrance, or adit, to the old iron mine. It has been blocked up for safety reasons. If you carry on you will follow the tramway almost to the top.

Over the footbridge.

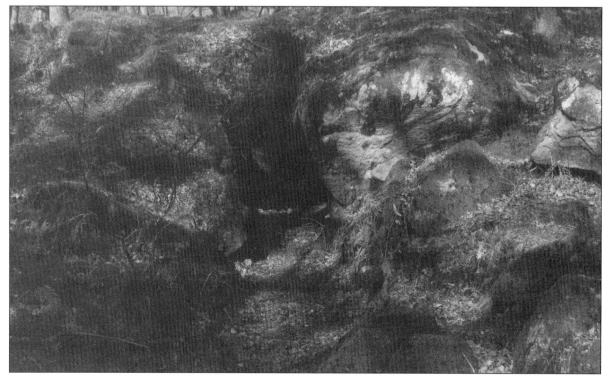

The entrance to the old iron mine.

The turn-off for the Devil's Rocks.

Stroll up the cobbled track past the turn-off to the Devil's Rocks.

Continue up to the left and turn at the top of the cobbled track; this leads onto the tramway.

Underfoot can be seen the granite rail sleepers as this winds its way past a curving pinnacle of rock on the left, then turn right and slightly downhill.

Part way down the slope is a track running up to the right. This is a distinctly straight and even uphill incline which was where two wagons were used on ropes to lower the granite blocks from the upper quarry onto the lower levels. The central part of this inclined track is wider to allow the two wagons to pass by each other.

Follow the tram track upwards, the other path takes you to Dewerstone Cottage and Goodameavy.

At the top can be found the remains of the cable brake housing and its central winch drum, which was used to slowly let the laden wagon down the hill. This consisted of two drums and a central pair of band brakes to balance the wagons, but this has since rotted away, leaving just the central shaft and a few retaining bands.

Beside the ruin is a level track with a discarded dressed stone on the side, leading across to the quarry itself and its extended spoil tip.

Just beyond the quarry is a small foot track to the left of the main track, leading up through the trees to the top of the Dewerstone Tor.

There are fine views at the top and there is the site of a Bronze-Age farmstead or settlement towards Wigford Down. The surrounding field wall can still be seen and as such, may also have been fortified. The rocks have a few inscriptions, including one to the poet Carrington, from Plymouth, who died on 2 September 1830.

The return is away from the quarry, to the south-east, so carefully pick the way down through the rocks, trees and roots to the top of the climbing rocks.

Keep clear of any steep, rocky edges.

The tracks lead down, veering to the right, and will pick up the other main track, which leads back to

The old tram track.

Pixie's Rock beside the tram track.

the bend at the top of the cobbled track and thence back to the start.

Route to the Devil's Rocks
Start as if you were going to the top of the Dewerstone. Halfway up the path, before the first bend, is a small signposted path to the right. If you take the right-hand path this will take you to the Devil's Rocks. Follow this path around the side of the hill, at a constant height to the river, to reach the Dewerstone area of large rocks.

Eventually the path reaches a large, rocky outcrop with an upper and lower path leading around it in the upstream direction. There is also another path veering uphill to the left, away from the main climbing area.

On the other side of the rocky outcrop lie the steps down to the open area under the main climbing faces.

From here, there are a few routes radiating upstream and uphill, but making a route up the river to Cadover is very difficult.

This is a very fine short stroll through the woods, and the path is very clear.

There are four main rock outcrops: the

Dewerstone Cottage and Goodameavy.

Dewerstone, Devil's Rock, Needle Buttress and, further upstream and set back a little, Raven Buttress.

The more popular routes up the climbing face include 'Climbers Club' (with variations), 'Central Groove' and 'Mucky Gulley'.

The following is a description of three of the many climbs. DO NOT attempt these, they are here just to

The remains of the cable brake housing.

A dressed granite stone.

The view from the top.

A stone showing the drill hole where the dynamite would have been inserted to break up the granite.

Carrington's obituary. The lettering has been picked out to make it more legible.

The view from the top of one of the outcrops.

show where the routes are. Always begin climbing only with a qualified and experienced climber.

Pinnacle Buttress
37m. Difficult.
Start up chimney, right to foot of buttress. Tend right, to reach ledge, below pinnacle, take bounding ridge right, to top.

Central Groove
55m. Mild Very Severe.
Steep 5m wall start at base of main groove. Awkward stance at 15 m – thread belays. Up groove to exit right, on sharp edge holds to good belay. Avoid overhang on left to upper top of meadow. Finish with the 6m chimney.

Climbers Club Direct
50m. Very Severe.
Start 6m right of central groove, to overhang and crack above to flake which is reached across wall (XS move). Join ordinary route. Follow groove to overhang, surmounted on left and belay.

Chimney up groove to follow Climbers Club ordinary route to top.

The return route of the stroll is back the same way to the bridge.

For those seeking a more adventurous path, continue up the granite path, up to the top, and the Iron-Age fort, then take the right-hand rough path around the top of the rocks, and, if very careful, scramble down around Raven Buttress. Seen from across the valley.

In 1960, a climber found a cup-sized Bronze-Age

Above and previous page: *The main climbing faces.*

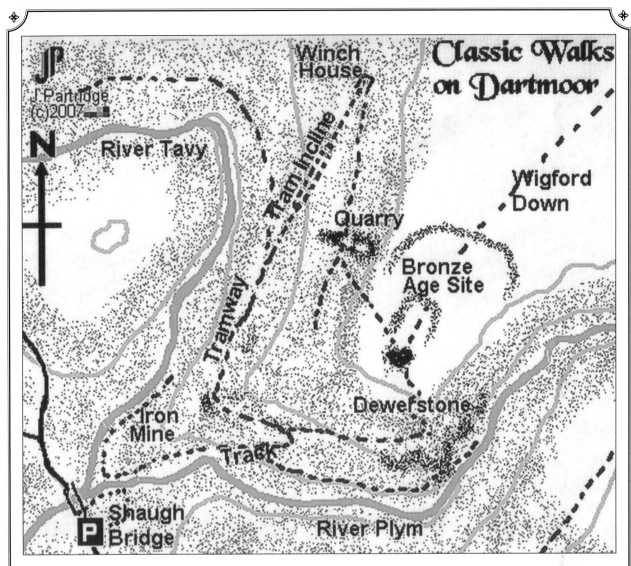

John's map of the routes.

A view of the outcrops from the other side of the river.

The author, on the right, being interviewed for 'The Legendary Trail', 17 June 2007.

drinking vessel near here.

At the top of the hill here are the remains of a small Iron-Age fort, or perhaps a fortressed farm from about 800 to 400BC.

Don Balkwill (aged 62)

This little story illustrates the influence of the internet. In June 2007 I was approached by a small production company who were thinking of bringing out a series of dvds about some of the better known Dartmoor legends. They had seen my website on Shaugh and asked me to take part. The project was to be called 'The Legendary Trail'. I met their production team on Sunday, 17 June 2007 at the base of the Dewerstone and they filmed me talking about my experiences living in the area. This ended up, after editing, as a 10 minute film clip. Sadly, they seem to have dropped the project and moved on to other things. However, that little bit of film came out as a video clip on the internet.

Not too long ago some friends and I were talking about unusual names and of course I have one of those, so we did a Google search on my name. On the first five pages of results that video clip appeared on 23 different video sites. Don't ask me why all the other sites had copied it, because I just don't know.

CHAPTER 10

Dewerstone Cottage

Graham Eagle, District Commissioner for Plymouth Scouts
Compiled from many different sources

Granite was not quarried on Dartmoor until the early 1800s. Before this, surface granite – known as 'moor-stone', was ample for all needs. Quarrying on the Dewerstone was in existence long before the railway, the granite being removed by horse-drawn vehicles.

In 1850 a quarrying firm (Johnson & Johnson), their hope of commercial expansion being raised by the building of the South Devon Tavistock Railway (SDTR), commenced operation. Johnson & Johnson, who later became the Haytor Granite Co., also ran the Foggintor quarries, and set about building a railway system to transport the granite across the Meavy to a siding alongside the main line.

Dewerstone Cottage was the counting house,

**WESTERN DAILY MERCURY
THURSDAY, 25th April, 1885
Page 1   Column 3**

Duerstone Cottage, Goodameavy, Duerstone Granite Quarries
Sale Monday, 4th May, 1885

MR P. HAMLEY is favoured with instructions from Mr. Webber, to SELL by AUCTION on the above premises on MONDAY, 4th May, 1885, the whole of the HOUSEHOLD FURNITURE contained therein, comprising trichord pianoforte in rosewood case, six iron French bedsteads, pair of palliasses, hair, wool, and spring mattresses, sets of mahogany drawers, dressing glasses, &c., &c., Kitchen and Cullinary Utensils and Effects.

Sale to Commence at Three p.m.

On View morning of Sale.

The earliest reference found to 'Duerstone' Cottage, in the Western Daily Mercury *of Thursday 25 April 1885.*

A postcard of Dewerstone Cottage posted in 1907. The notice on the door reads 'Teas served and local water supplied'.

A photoraph developed from a glass plate showing Dewerstone Cottage some time in the period 1910–20.

stables and smithy for the granite railway system. Two quarries, 200ft above the cottage, were connected by a narrow-gauge track. Along the side of the highest part of the tramway are some rejected pieces of nearly finished dressed stone. Descent to the lower track was achieved by way of an inclined plane railway. The inclined plane is 400yds (365m) long with a fall of 200ft (61m) and a gradient of 1:6. A counterbalance system was used whereby full

trucks descending pulled up empty trucks for filling. A winding house at the top of the incline controlled the cable system. The ruins of the winding house and the sets for mounting the sleepers are still visible today. Near the top the rows of sleeper blocks are very prominent, as is the spoil of a badger set which has piled up over the incline in the 100 years or so since it was last used. Further quarries were situated on the lower track, which was of standard gauge. In two of the quarries the bosses for mounting cranes can still be seen. The lower track ran past the cottage, over Blacklands Brook, through the gate (Penns Gate) and cutting and across a bridge and an embankment. Here the line should have crossed the Meavy but this single-span bridge was never completed.

In 1857 negotiations were in hand with the SDTR but no final agreement seems to have been reached. Wayleave was, however, paid to Sir Massey Lopes for removal of granite across his land. In 1863 the building of the branch line was under way, but in 1865 the company went bankrupt. The firm abandoned the project, having used most of the quarry's production for the construction work involved. It is difficult to imagine now what the area would look like had the quarrying continued. Much of the granite that formed the embankment was removed in 1952 by Plymouth Corporation and used as part of the construction of the Lopwell Dam on the Tavy.

The cottage became a dwelling, on lease from Goodameavy Manor, and the occupants sold teas and water to walkers who travelled out from Plymouth on the railway (by now the GWR) to Shaugh Platform.

This situation continued until about 1952, when the last occupants (Mr and Mrs Legg) moved out. (Before the Leggs the occupants were the Northmores.) The cottage then gradually became derelict and fell into ruin.

Biographical Notes:
Mrs Mabel Legg (née Sercombe) was born in 1907 in Venton. Her family moved to Shaugh Prior when Mabel was quite young. In October 1929 Mabel married Charles Legg in Plympton St Mary. During the Second World War the couple lived in the Dewerstone Cottage and Mabel delivered mail from Roborough to Meavy and Clearbrook. They used part of the cottage as a tearoom and supplied cream teas to thousands of visitors to Shaugh Woods who used the train to get to Shaugh Halt. In 1956 Mabel was the canteen cook at Shaugh Prior Primary School, where she worked until retiring in 1967. She celebrated her 100th birthday in February 2007.

Mrs Legg appears in a 1956 school photograph in Chapter 2 (see page 29). Her nephew, Graham (Nobby) Clarke, who attended the school, is second from the left on the top row.

The National Trust acquired the estate in 1960, part gifted from the Treasury in lieu of death duties.

Dewerstone Cottage in 1962 in ruins, just before the rebuild carried out by Devon Scouts.

With the aid of local authority and ministry grants and thanks to such generous supporters of Devon Scouting as Viscount Amory, the Northcott Devon Foundation, the Headquarters of the Boy Scouts' Association and other friends who preferred to remain anonymous, the derelict building was converted into an adventure and training centre.

The centre was opened in 1965 by Viscount Amory, Mr Charles Chapman (County Commissioner) and the Revd Sampson (County Executive Committee Chairman). The lease with the National Trust was in the name of Mr Crispin Gill, although this later passed to the Scout Association Trust.

Dewerstone Cottage, c.1983.

Peter Ashton (aged 69)

My name is Peter Ashton and I am 69 years old. During the war from about 1942 and up to about 1950 we lived in a little hut that my father built at Goodameavy. We had one main living-room, a large bedroom with two bunks for me and my sisters and another bedroom for my mother and father.

Our hut was built backing up onto the rocks of the raised tramway just before the bridge over the river. It was down the bottom of the path from the Dewerstone Cottage.

We had no gas or electricity. We did have a hurricane lamp and a Tilley lamp which we used to pump up to

keep the pressure up. We had a Primus for cooking and we also had a couple of wick oil lamps with the long glass funnel on the top. We had an Everready radio which ran off an accumulator. My father used to get the accumulator charged in Plymouth, although I didn't realise that at the time – well, little boys don't, do they? They just accept that things are always there.

We used to get water from the river. When you went to get it you always pointed the opening of the bucket downstream to prevent the muck and bits getting into the bucket. We lived at the hut for six or seven years, I

113

Dewerstone Cottage in the winter of 1987.

Dewerstone Cottage, 2007.

suppose, but not all the time; only to get away from Plymouth. The dockyard was always being bombed, and we were certainly at the hut through the school holidays and during weekends; it depended on the bombing. We stayed there sometimes for weeks and weeks. We did all the things that little boys do: bows and arrows, cricket, adventures, climbing – you name it, we did it. There were three children, my two sisters and myself. I had another brother but he was evacuated.

We didn't go to school locally, we went to our usual school in Plymouth as much as possible during term time because father had to work in Plymouth. Father had a car, a little Morris 8, but he left it at the hut most of the time because petrol was on rationing. We used to travel back and forward by train. At the end of the war the car went back to Plymouth. We lived at the bottom of Milehouse in Plymouth, near the Plymouth Argyle football ground.

When we moved away I suppose I was about 12. We still kept the hut as a holiday cottage until we had to pull it down when they were building Lopwell Dam. They wanted the granite that was there.

I remember those days with pleasure. It was a wonderful childhood.

Peter Ashton with one of his sisters, c.1948.

Goodameavy Bridge, c.1920.

From top: *The Moorland residence, the Moorland Guest House, finally the Moorland Hotel*

❖ CHAPTER 11 ❖

Wotter

The village of Wotter really only came into existence in 1906. Prior to that date there were only two dwelling-houses and a farm between Shaugh Prior and Lee Moor. As Arthur Selleck tells us, houses were needed for the workmen employed by the Dartmoor China Clay Co. during its expansion, so the company had them built.

Malcolm Clarke (aged 60)

The Methodist Church at Wotter had its final service on Sunday, 22 April 2007, and was sold to become a Christian Outreach Centre. Wotter is now [2008] left without any kind of public hall, community shop or hotel of any kind.

The Moorland Hotel was originally the Moorland Guest House; the change took place in the early '60s and I worked there at weekends and after school between 1961 and 1967. About 1962/63 the owner, Mr Ben Trethewey, changed it from a guest-house to a hotel because, as a guest-house, only residents could use the bar; when it became a hotel the public could use it too. He then had many more customers who could just drop in for a drink, as they did to the White Thorn. The residential trade died after the Second World War and he would not have been able to survive if he had not changed. Prior to the change his family, being Methodist, had many Methodists stay each summer as paying guests for weeks at a time, and no alcohol was the rule of the day before the war. When he changed to

licensed premises the rest of the family pulled out of the business and there was a small rift – soon patched up, of course. He and his wife and family had to live in the new age which was dawning. He sold it as a flourishing hotel but I cannot quite remember when. I have no knowledge at all of present ownership or what it is like today. [At the time of writing the hotel is closed and is awaiting sale to a developer – DB]

My mother was a Sercombe and her family was closely associated with Wotter. I was born at the bottom of Collard Lane in a bungalow called Collard Bungalow and spent hours on the farm next door with the Vincent family at Lower Collard Farm and also with the Rowe family at Coldstone Farm. These farms are very old,

Dartmoor Cottages, Wotter, in the very early days.

A Sunday-school outing from Wotter. c.1931.

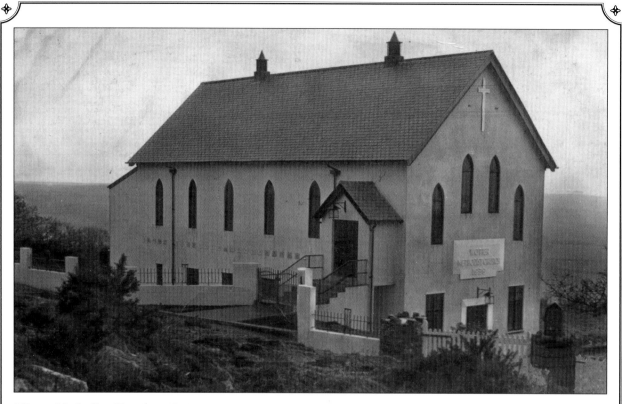

Wotter Methodist Church, c.1940.

Above: *Elsie and Ted Daw's wedding at the Moorland Hotel, 1941.*

Left: *Elsie Daw with baby John Daw outside the Oaks, 1944.*

Olive and Ernest May at their 60th wedding anniversary in the old Lee Moor Hall.

with Lower Collard eleventh century, if I recall correctly, and Coldstone sixteenth century. Truelove Farm is close by, but the two Dennis brothers went to live in Shaugh.

My cousin, Ann Sercombe, was the daughter of Frank Sercombe, who was Deputy Manager of the clay works at Lee Moor in the 1970s and '80s.

Norman May (aged 74)

I am now 74 years old; I grew up in Wotter and lived in Dartmoor Cottages. During the Second World War my father was in the Home Guard. There were an anti-aircraft gun and a searchlight in a field above the school. One day a German aeroplane was shot down. I found a piece of the Perspex canopy. There were also three Americans, based in Lee Moor near the school, who lived in tents. My father kept chickens and I used to visit the Americans and they would swap their food for eggs, which they didn't have. Sometimes they would give me a meal, or perhaps some bacon to take home. Buses from Plymouth were parked in Lee Moor during the night to prevent them being destroyed in the blitz of Plymouth.

I went to school first at Shaugh Prior, and then at Lee Moor. I don't know why my parents changed my school. I remember at Shaugh School the dentist used to visit a couple of times a year. The first time I saw him I had four teeth extracted and I was given an injection first and then had to wait for it to take effect. I was only about five or six years old at the time.

In the winter it seemed we always had snow, often blizzards. The first time, I can recall, my father, Mr Phillips, Mr Walters and Mr Skelly linked arms and formed a shield, and we all walked behind them. As far as I can remember there was my brother Gordon,

myself, Ron Skelly, Joan Walters, Sid and Bill Phillips and Bill Lillicrap.

When I was older and the snow had fallen in Wotter, if it was very thick on the ground my brother and I used to get out the sledge that my father had made for us and would then go around the village and take orders for bread. We then pulled the sledge about five miles to Plympton St Mary's and go to the bakery at the top of Gaslight Hill. The baker would put the loaves of bread into a hessian sack. We would tie the sack to the sledge and drag it back to Wotter and distribute the bread to the villagers, who would pay us for fetching it.

In the village there was a shop owned by Harold Wilcox, a Post Office, which was in the front room of No. 24 Dartmoor Cottages and run by Mrs Tucker, and at the rear of the chapel was a surgery. It was just two rooms and was held every Friday morning. The doctor, Dr Bull, would take the prescriptions to Plympton, and the medicine would come up on the bus in the evening. My mother was a wonderful person and was always helping the neighbours. If any of the children were ill their parents would take them to my mother, and she would diagnose what was wrong with them – things like measles and chickenpox. She would then ring the doctor and explain what was wrong and he would just write a prescription for the patient without seeing them.

A friend of mine, David Kinsman, who was the son of the blacksmith, Mark Kinsman, was quite a character. I remember he used to go out wearing two pairs of trousers, one on top of the other. This would be during the evening and he would walk up the bank of the River Meavy until he found a secluded spot. He would then snare a salmon and put it down his trousers between the two layers so that no one could see that he had a fish there. It hung from his waist by its tail. He often gave my Mum some of the salmon.

Every morning, Mrs Skelly from Wotter Farm would arrive in a pony and trap with two churns of milk and a pint dipper. People would come out with their jugs for their milk. If Mr Skelly had a runt pig he would give it to my mother to be reared. When it reached the required size Mr Squires from Lee Moor, who did all the slaughtering for the parish, would come and kill the pig. He would then cut it up, and it would be put in a lead-lined trough using layers of pork and salt, which came in large blocks, because there were no refrigerators and freezers in those days. At Christmas we usually had a goose, which my mother had also reared beforehand.

Olive and Ernest May
described by their Daughter-in-law, Tracey May

The picture (see previous page) shows only a few of their grandchildren, because they had 21 grandchildren in all and I cannot count how many great and great-great-grandchildren they have produced (I would need an abacus as I do not have enough toes and fingers). I think it is probably half of the population of Shaugh, Wotter, Lee Moor and Cornwood.

Olive was known by some of the residents of Wotter as Gran May, and as Auntie Oll (Olive) by others. If someone had a sick child the doctor in Plympton would tell them to ask Gran May what she thought it was because she had raised nine children herself and then had a hand in raising all the grandchildren. Gran May would say, 'It looks like mumps or chickenpox etc,' and the doctor would say, 'If that's what she thinks it is then that's good enough for me; she has seen it all'. He would then send a prescription up on the next bus.

She actually gave birth to her twins all on her own because the midwife didn't get there in time. Both of the twins were in excess of 7lb each at birth (ouch! is what I say). She was a wonderful and special person whom everyone loved and I was proud to have her as my mother-in-law. She was a big lady with a big character, with a big heart, who played a big part in the community of Wotter. She was loved by all who knew her.

Sadly, she died in 1986. The chapel was absolutely packed for her funeral; they had to move the screen at the back to make room for everyone. They were even lined up on the steps outside.

Dad was lovely, too. He was a strict Methodist but had a heart of gold (I could wind him around my little

Olive and Ernest's nine children: Gordon, Norman, Dorothy, David, Daphne, John, Stuart, Margaret and Pauline, 1948.

Olive and Ernest (third from left, front row) at an old people's Christmas party.

The wedding of Daphne and Ken Goss in the mid-1960s. The two tall girls at the front are Pauline and Margaret May1 and between them is Linda Reed.

finger). He died 13 weeks after mum. Although he was not in very good health they said the only diagnosis they could make for his demise was a broken heart. Mum was 75 and Dad was 81.

Tracey May (aged 62)

I worked at Bass Charringtons at Marsh Mills with a girl from Wotter, Dawn Legg. She and her family invited me to spend part of the Christmas festivities with them. We went to the White Thorn at Shaugh Prior for a drink and Norman was in there. He was playing a game with dice which they called euchre (pronounced yooker); he asked if we would like to play but I declined. Unbeknown to me, Norman was a professional folksinger who sang under the name of 'Nibs May'. He used to sing all over the UK and Ireland and even sang to the royal family at the Royal Albert Hall. He also had a regular spot on Westward Television here in Plymouth. I probably used to watch him on television, not realising I would one day marry him!

Anyway, back to the story. We had to sit next to him and his friends because the place was so crowded, and when they finished their game he challenged me to a game of darts. I accepted the challenge but said I wasn't very good when in actual fact it was a favorite pastime of mine and I was really quite good. Needless to say, I beat him, which didn't seem to impress him so he went back to his friends. Dawn and I decided to go to the Moorland Hotel in Wotter and, as we were about to leave, Norman asked where we were going. Before long guess who turned up at the Moorland too? Norman bought us supper and asked me for a date. It must have been love at first sight because we got married in the May of the following year at Shaugh Church. We had the reception at the old Lee Moor Hall. We also had an evening reception at the White Thorn. Norman's friends from the world of folk turned up and we had a great time with singing/music and dancing – oh, and of course, plenty of drinking (as you do, hee! hee!).

After we were married Norman gave up singing because we wanted a family and Norman didn't want to be traveling all the time. He took a job as a driver/courier for a coach firm. I continued with Bass Charringtons for a while before starting our family. We

Outside the Lee Moor Public Hall, at Norman and Tracey May's reception, 25 May 1968.

Wotter May Fayre, 1951. Could those two little pixies be Margaret and Pauline May? That May family gets everywhere!

then went into the licensed trade for a few years and combined this with a very successful landscaping business until Norman had to retire due to a disability. I continued as a manager at a large public house until and then went as a manager for a GP practice and stayed there until I retired. I was contacted by a surgery three months later and asked to help them raise their income. Soon after that I was contacted by yet another surgery for the same reason. I am now back as a practice manager at that surgery in Plymstock. I must need my head testing.

Norman and I have been married for over 40 years. Do I get a gold medal for that? Mind you, as compensation we have two daughters, Jacquie and Sarah, and six grandchildren, Shayne (21), Jodie (19), Kaylie (18), Sheri-lea (16), Shannan (12) and Kelsey (12). We have *also been blessed with two great-grandchildren, Lara (22 months) and Ethan (20 months), and they are adorable.*

David Tyrrell-Collins (aged 65)

Below the Moorland Hotel and the house called Sungarth is an area called the Ruts. On the right, as you approach the Ruts are two bungalows, 'Innisfree' and 'Rockholm'. The land where these now stand was bought by Ernest Collins in the 1920s and a small property was built there which was given to his daughter Theodora as a twenty-first birthday present in 1931.

There is a mention of the white china clay waste path that led to Innisfree in Eden Philpott's novel, The Three Brothers, *published in 1927.*

Originally the bungalow was used as a weekend escape from Plymouth. Sandwiches were packed for a trip on the Princetown line to Shaugh Station and a walk to Wotter. This little pied-à-terre became less used when work as an actress took Theodora to London, where she was training, or working, with Joyce Grenfell in the Royal Albert Hall, and, after marriage, to Sussex.

During the early part of the Second World War Theodora returned to Plymouth and, through contacts with the Astor/Grenfell family, she adopted an illegitimate boy named David in 1943. Soon after this buildings on the opposite side of the road were demolished. This was followed in the next raid by a direct hit by a bomb that didn't go off. The bomb travelled right through the house and ended up pointing at my cot in the cellar. A rapid relocation took place and the family settled in Innisfree. A bathroom and annexe were rapidly added and Innisfree took on its final shape.

The whole family lived in the bungalow until 1948, when Theodora sold the property back to her father for £800 and bought a house in Wales, where she moved with her husband Felix, a new baby called Christina and me.

I was always treated by Ernest and Georgina Collins as their own grandson and as a consequence I returned to Wotter on every holiday. During the Easter Holidays I spent much time 'bob-a-jobbing' in Wotter, Lee Moor and Shaugh and, due to the generosity of local people, I always won the award for the largest amount of cash collected within the Scout troop when I returned to Wales.

In the early 1950s another bungalow called Rockholm was built in the garden of Innisfree for relatives Clara and Margaret Haines. All the people that assisted in the building were over 60.

Margaret Haines was District Nurse in the area for many years. The house was legally transferred to them in 1959.

Georgina and Ernest Collins were teachers, but he was previously a master cabinetmaker. Ernest died later in 1959 and soon after Innisfree was sold to Charles and Mabel Legg. It now [2008] belongs to Andrew Loosely.

Ernest Collins, 1955.

Theodora Collins, an actress in early life, then trained as a speech therapist.

I returned to Devon in 1997 and stayed in the Moorland Hotel until I bought a house in Dousland. I live in Torquay at the time of writing.

The story of the Dewerstone legends reminded me of one escapade when I had decided to ride out on my pony. I always started at my grandparent's house, Innisfree, in Wotter. The previous day I had been told the Dewerstone story about the rider who killed unbaptised babies. It was probably told to me as a cruel tease when the lads learnt that I wasn't baptised. However, I can't think of anyone who would be likely to have done this. I didn't really believe the story, but some doubts were still there. I had been brought up by Quakers so I was not baptised and that didn't help.

Against my grandparents' wishes I decided to ride to Whiteworks, which is the old tin mine south of Princetown. The weather, as it often does on Dartmoor, 'clamped', that is the mist and low cloud came down and visibility was just a matter of feet.

I was just 12 and got totally lost and I must admit the

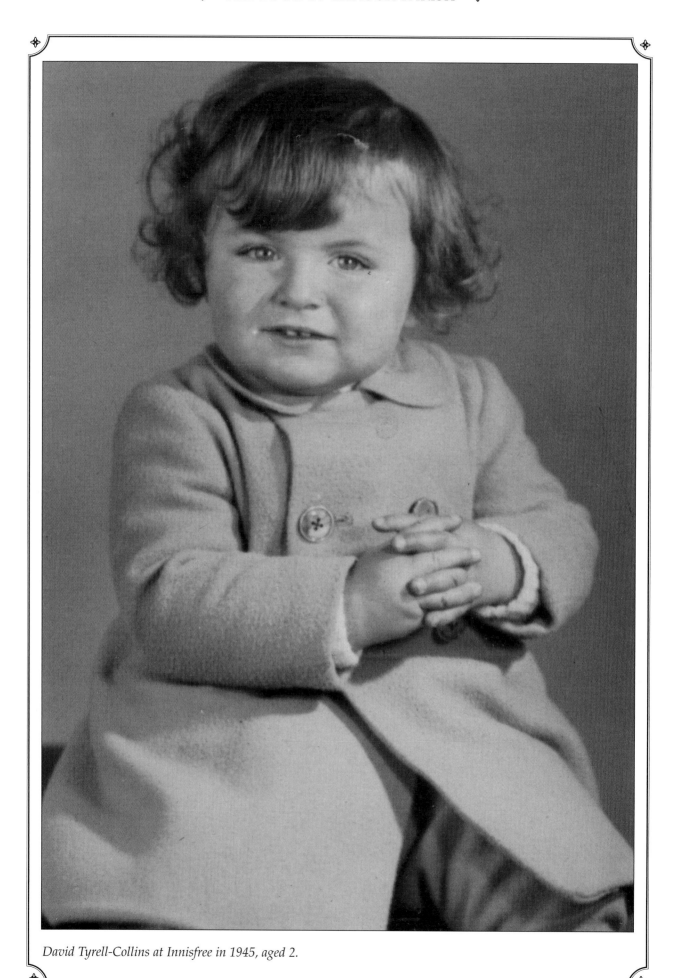

David Tyrell-Collins at Innisfree in 1945, aged 2.

David and sister Christina Meade at Innisfree, 1954.

Dewerstone story had frightened me. I was out for, I guess, four or five hours. In the end it was my reliable pony, Pegasus, which my grandparents had bought for me from a farmer at Lower Shaugh, who saved the day. The farmer's name was Fred and he and his Scottish wife lived in the original White Thorn. We paid 11 guineas for the pony which was later sold to the Royal Marines as their mascot. I was very upset about this but my grandparents' retirement budget was not enough for such a luxury.

Pegasus brought me back over Collard Tor and I was greeted by the Plympton bobby and the Royal Marines

because by this time my grandfather had raised the alarm. In spite of all the fuss we somehow managed to keep it quiet. I think the only people who knew were the Trethewys, who were family friends and close neighbours at the Moorland Guest House, Miss Yabsley the post lady and May (her surname escapes me), who ran the Post Office at Wotter at the back of the Methodist Chapel. For once the grapevine had failed – it must have been a first, for even Andrew Loosley (May's nephew) didn't know until I told him. It was just one of the things that happened to me because I remember the risks I took climbing the Dewerstone – and also

David in the Scouts in the mid-'50s.

Georgina and Ernest Collins with Clara Haines in the garden of Innisfree, 1953.

Sheep's Tor – the hard way. Mind you, never on the same day. I look at them now and shrink at the thought (I now get dizzy on tip-toe).

Lenore Hicks

My mother's name was Audrey Heyden and she was a teacher at Wotter School. She went to Exeter College (as it was then), so I think the earliest date she might have taught at Wotter would have been 1925. I have a vague memory of something my mother said that there was only one classroom, and I wonder if she taught all ages (up to 11, I suppose) in that one room. I think she lodged there during the week, as her home was in Tavistock. The journey was either by train or walking to the main Plymouth/Tavistock road to catch a bus. She later went on to teach at Tavistock Primary School and married in 1932.

In Chapter 7 there is mention made of Fred Jefferys

Wotter Primary School, 1921. The school closed in 1931.

Wotter Red Cross. At back: Betty Walters; left to right, middle row: Mavis Clarke, Diane Antcliffe, Winifred Grimes, Judy Kingwell, Ralph Kingwell, ?, Mervyn Pundsack, John Kennard, Ian ?, Maureen Antcliffe, Roy Lillicrap; front row: Anthony Pundsack, Bryan Pullyblank, Mrs Lillian Jeffries, Joy Doidge, Una Pundsack, Jill Kingwell.

A Christmas party at Wotter schoolrooms. Lillian Jeffrey, in uniform, is sitting next to the vicar.

junr, who married Lillian (see photographs of the Red Cross and of the Christmas party at Wotter schoolrooms), who had previously been married to a white tea planter in India.

The following is Arthur Selleck's account of how his family restarted clay-mining operations in Wotter.

Arthur Selleck
supplied by Malcolm Norman
(see page 153)

The Bray family band mentioned in the Lee Moor part of this book [see Chapter 12 – DB] was not related to that of Captain John Bray, who became works manager at the time of my grandfather. Captain John Diamond Cobbledick passed from this scene of action in 1891. The above Captain John Bray was appointed to take his place and my father, Christopher Robert Henry Selleck, lately returned from America but previously trained at Lee Moor, became second in the management. The senior of the firm Martin Bros, Mr William Martin, also died about this time and so the old order changed. At the turn of the century there was a greatly increased demand for china clay, and investors were very keen to acquire 'setts'. The Lee Moor group was producing ever-increasing quantities. The main Lee Moor pit, then 40 acres in the area, the Chalwichtown pit and the New Whitehill Yeo pit were then in full production, but the Wotter pit, on the western side, had been abandoned. In September 1901 my father reopened Wotter. It caused rather more than a 'nine days' wonder' that he should have the audacity to restart works declared uneconomic, redundant and worked out by his former employers. They said he was heading for disaster and they were nearly right. The epic struggle began. Father Chris, C.R.H. or Cap'n Chrissy, as he was variously known, packed his belongings on the carts behind Shamrock – the old grey mare – and Tommy horse (the latter a family friend for many years after) and trundled over Highboro' Hill together with nine of us – six boys and three girls. Mother, who was the most wonderful homemaker, soon settled us in at Wotter House. For a

time we shared the house with the Elliot family, who went to Perks Farm, Shaugh Prior. My father, who soon found his slender capital stretched to capacity, acquired a secondhand traction engine and trucks from a local firm of brick makers to haul the clay to the railway station. There were a few other oddments of equipment; then with about four or five men and his own family he got down to the job. Then trouble came on trouble. As already indicated, china-clay production depends on adequate supplies of water. The water for the group Cholwichtown, Whitehill Yeo, Lee Moor and Wotter was drawn from the upper reaches of the Cad near Trowlesworthy. We found the lifeline was cut – the stream had been diverted at Lee Moor. Means were then devised to collect water on our own limited watershed. Ponds (reservoirs) had to be constructed to try to meet the situation.

Next of the major problems was to be that of transport. The roads over Dartmoor in those days were little more than bridle tracks, and to drive a traction engine laden with two ten-ton trucks of clay was asking too much and we were thus landed into trouble with the Plympton Rural District Council. Our local neighbours also. In seeking alternative routes we tried the roads to Bickleigh, Cornwood and Plympton railway stations. The law required us to employ a man with a red flag to walk in front of the trucks. I remember one memorable morning going out to play from the school at Lee Moor when we all rushed out to the road to see our engine, complete with guard and red flag, coming down the road towards Tory Coombe. Quite an impressive crowd had gathered when Captain Bray, acting under orders, forbade the driver, my brother Chris, to proceed any further over that section of the road. But necessity calls for desperate measures and after what was mostly unintelligible conversation, Chris, 'naughty boy', after opening the cylinder drains which enveloped the Captain in a cloud of steam, drove on his desperate journey. The Captain, when thus forced to retire, was heard to remark, 'They'm doin' it in defiance'. Needless to say, the name of that engine from that time was Defiance. However, a few years afterwards the two families celebrated the marriage of my brother Chris to Captain Bray's daughter, Mabel, so time healed the breach. We then stuck to the Cornwood Road, but what a shambles! My father now had to face a hostile District Council and when challenged as to what he proposed to do about this 4–5 miles of road he promptly replied that he proposed to repair it. To say the least this seemed an impossible task, but we tackled it and literally thousands of tons of stone – 'Stent', as it was locally called – were raised by us and hauled and rolled in by our engines over the section from Wotter to Cornwood, free of charge to the RDC. With such a traffic strain, traction engines breakdowns were frequent and it seemed as if the limit must soon be reached. One evening, on his way home through Lee Moor, my father was led to go and see a bedridden Jack Quest. Jack had not been able to meet at the Sunday morning eight o'clock prayer meeting for some time, so father felt it his duty to see him. Jack relates the conversation:

'Well Chris how is it with you?'

'Not too good Jack, a bit of a headache (small wonder). Engine broke down today.'

'You're going through it Chris, wish I could help. Never mind Chris (reaching for his Bible) read in the 37th psalm.'

So he read as far as verse 25: 'I have been young and now I am old, yet have I not seen the righteous forsaken nor his seed begging bread.'

Said Chris to me some time after, 'I don't know exactly why but he seemed to have a lump in his throat and couldn't read on for a little while.'

I knew and we all knew that things had become so tight that we had not to stave off poverty much longer. Frugality and thrift had been the order of five long years, but he read on, prayed on, and worked on, he was not forsaken and those who knew them, will know that his seed are not begging bread. But how dark was that hour before the dawn. Only those who went through it will ever know. We members of the family were variously employed on jobs whereby we could contribute most to the common good. My brother John trained at Lee Moor in all branches of the smith's trade. In addition to making necessary ironwork for the development of the works, he continued to earn something extra by making and repairing implements and shoeing horses for local farmers. There was no eight-hour limit to days. Chris had to spend most of his time as a mechanical engineer, repairing engines, designing gadgets to make things run more smoothly on the works. Will, at 15 years of age, went on the traction as a driver. I have known him work the 24 hours around the clock if it happened that we had to load a cargo boat. Problems piled up as we proceeded, one of our particular problems at this time was how best to use the water at our disposal; the old Cornish way was to let the water trickle over the top of the 'slope' (clay bed), having broken the surface with 'dubbers' (wide leading picks) at an angle of about 45° from the bottom of the pit to the top edge of the 'stope'. One man would break a 'strake' of clay 10–15 feet in width. We found at Wotter that the 'stope' was getting very thin and the clay tough (not friable). The water would run clear instead of taking away the clay in solution. My father, who by this time had been elected to Plympton Council, came home from Plympton having made a few observations on the pressure needed to send water from a fire hose to the top of a burning house and expressed the opinion to my brothers that water pressure was the answer to our washing problems. Chris got to work on this and I remember the water was impounded in earthenware 2.5 inch drainpipes for quite a long distance, then fed into iron pipes on the lower levels, where pressure was highest, making the best of the materials (a job lot) at his disposal. The experiment proved successful and established the method in common use today. Within two

years we were repeating the stroam by centrifugal pumps at 100lb pressure per square inch. Thus again, 'necessity was the mother of invention', or shall we say application. The above-related incident took place in 1905. My father had formed a limited company, Selleck & Sons Ltd, but economic necessity made confusion worse confounded and our policy was shaped accordingly.

Then suddenly, on a Sunday morning, came the answer to our prayers. For some unaccountable reason (to us) Captain Chrissy was called out from the Sunday morning service at Lee Moor. Was someone ill? What had happened?

What happened was this: Messrs Punchard, Stewart and Vivion, three successful speculators in Malayan rubber, were looking for a China clay 'sett' and wished to do business with my father on the spot. He respectfully but firmly refused to do this on the Lord's Day, but arranged to meet them on the morrow. They met, the die was cast, the deal was made, and a new era for Wotter began in 1906. Selleck & Sons Ltd went into voluntary liquidation and the Dartmoor China Clay Co. was formed. This marked the beginning of a great advancement. China clay (kaolin) was found to have much wider potential uses than merely as a filling agent in cotton manufacturing, papermaking and all the actual making of china or pottery. Chemical research proved the possibility of the production of colloidal clays was in ready demand. Wotter was soon producing this particular brand in this field known as 'Catalpo'. Dries were constructed at Marsh Mills, near Plymouth, and a pipeline laid to convey the clay in solution. The scheme initiated by my father obviated the further use of expensive mechanical transport. There was, of course, a period of years during which we had to continue hauling the clay over the long and tortuous route to Cornwood Station. This great burst of activity made it necessary to build houses for the workmen, and thus we witnessed the birth of a village; previously only three houses existed between Shaugh Prior and Lee Moor. They were Wotter Farm, Wotter House and Collard Tor. The period 1906–14 was one of great prosperity in the industry, and in the Lee Moor district all the pits were in full production – Chaldwichtown, Whitehill Yeo, Lee Moor, Wotter, Hemerdon, Smithhanger, Headon, and Shaugh Lake. It will be seen from the above that the Selleck family made many contributions to the clay industry. A summary of these would include the following:

1. The use of road transport, i.e. the steam engine, to convey the clay to the railhead at Cornwood Station.
2. The patenting of the Selleck (second son) patent steam cylindrical valve, which was an improvement on the slide valve fitted to the Aveling engine first used.
3. The use in 1905 of a pressurised water system to extract the clay. The shortage of water necessitated the reuse of the supply. This was the origin of the present system of centrifugal monitors, and even at this early

Fred Peters on his dumper truck in the mid- to late '40s.

Fred Peters worked at Wotter clay works driving a dumper truck. This photograph would appear to have been taken in the mid to late '40s because one of the men leaning against the dumper seems to be a prisoner of war. He worked there up until about 1956 and lived in the Kiln cottage at Shaugh Bridge.

stage pressure of 100lb per square inch was achieved.
4. About 1906 the Dartmoor China Clay Co. was formed with C.R.H. Selleck and sons as managers. Will Selleck, third son, later became the sole manager and continued in that capacity for approximately 25 years. For the first time ever clay was piped. The pipe ran from the Wotter works to Marsh Mills and is still in existence today.

5. Shortly after the First World War the fifth son, Claude Selleck, moved to Cornwall and at the age of 15 took over the running of Carbis clay works, followed by Great Treverbyn. His main contribution to the industry was the devising of a process for bleaching clay. This proved extremely valuable and, after considerable negotiation, it was purchased by English Clays, Lovering Pochin & Co. (ECLP), and Claude Selleck became a director of that company. This had far-reaching results, as Selleck Nicholls was taken over at this time and consequently the parent company found itself involved in the post-war housing crisis which Selleck Nicholls's 'Cornish Unit' did so much to solve.

As is well known, the then Minister of Housing, Aneurin Bevan, leant heavily on Claude Selleck to enable his housing target to be reached, and when this was achieved a knighthood was bestowed on John Keay, chairman of the parent company.

View of Lee Moor, 1989.

Pupils of Lee Moor School, 1956.

✦ CHAPTER 12 ✦

Lee Moor

Phil Kerswell (aged 62)

I was born in Lee Moor at No. 10 Broad Oaks on the last day of September 1945.

I believe my Dad, who was in the RAF, was still off in the war somewhere. He was obviously the hero in my life and will always be. I went to school in Lee Moor. The headmistress was Miss Cann and the other teacher was Miss Carbines.

I remember my classmates Adrienne Friendship, her brother Derek (Admiral) and her older brother Malcolm (Rocket). They were one of the first families to have a TV in the village. We boys used to wait patiently in the village for Saturday evening, when they used to show 'The Lone Ranger'. We were allowed to go into their home and watch the programme, and Adrienne's mum, Mrs Friendship, would give us biscuits.

Other classmates were Michael (Sammy) Squires and Rodney and Tony Squires, his brothers.

There were my cousins, Bobby and Deirdre Phillips and Vivienne Phillips; Hilary Selleck, Cheryl and Keith Ford, Valerie and Ralph Windsborough, also cousins; Clive Friendship, Barry Selleck, Janet Roberts, Romaine Broome, Valerie Poynter, Michael Quest and many more who evade me.

My sister Lynda used to appear in the pantos all the time. She was a tap dancer, as were all the other girls. I once appeared as the cat in Puss in Boots. Apart from that brief experience I don't remember much about it, except for sitting in the audience ogling the legs. The famous panto figures in my time were Gordon Lillicrap, Michael Mudge, Ruth Howard, Deidre Phillips, Bert Ryder, Ken Armstrong, and my step-mum, Doreen Beer.

In the summer, when I was between 6 and 12 years old, we used to walk to Cadover Bridge to swim and try and get back in time for tea. There were normally a couple of mums with us, but I remember doing it with a

Tony Squires and Bryan Pullyblank in pantomime.

Puss in Boots, 1957. *Joyce Butcher (née Lillicrap), who provided this photograph, is second from the right, kneeling.*

A cart-horse pulling a carnival float.

crowd of us a few times and burning furze bushes on the way home. You probably know, they give off a splendid column of smoke and crackle quite satisfyingly.

We lived in Long Row initially and the toilets were at the other end of the garden and one had to be seriously ill to escape the long walk just before bedtime. I used to go with my sister and often we stopped halfway, did our business and scurried back to the warm house.

We then move to Boringdon Cottages, No. 8 I think. The toilet was just as far away and just as scary, but there was no garden to stop halfway in.

My dad was a good footballer and was captain of the village team for several years.

He then went onto the committee and it was natural that I followed on. I played for Lee Moor for several

years until we moved away from the village to Parkland Farm, which is between Lee Moor and Cornwood.

Here's a bit of scandal. I'm not sure which year it happened, but one summer's evening I was on my way home for tea and I stopped in the stables which were just next to the public hall. I met Tony Squires, Gary Pope and Derek Friendship. We were discussing football practice, which was after tea. Anyway, I went home and after tea started off to the football pitch. On my way there the stables were on fire. It was the biggest fire ever in the village and most of the stables were burnt badly. I remember the fire brigade with the big hoses and the crowds of people. People were talking about it for years. BUT I KNOW.

The carnival was always the big event of the year. ECLP used to bring the big cart horses in a cattle van and the carnival queen and her princesses were paraded around the village.

This was a big event, all us kids were dressed up and some of the dads and mums, and it was a really splendid day. We used to look forward to it almost as much as Christmas. There were toffee apples, candy floss and all manner of things for small kids. The Co-op was the only shop in the village and I remember my Uncle Ron was the manager. I used to go with the ration coupons and get groceries for Mum. Our Co-op number was 1696 and when I went home I was always quizzed as to whether the number was written in the book. It was for a dividend I think, with which the customers once a year had a few free items.

Just down from the Co-op was a small shop which was

Lee Moor AFC team, 1950.

Lee Moor AFC team, 1954.

Lee Moor AFC team, 1965.

Lee Moor AFC, winners of the Plymouth Combination Champions League One, 1966. Left to right, back row: Stuart May, Graham Baskerville, Rodney Squires, Bill May, Dave Hayden, Clive Friendship, Ralph Kingwell, Ken Armistead; front row: Dave Andrew, Mike Perkins, Rob Wall, Herbie Bazely, Tony James.

a saddlery or shoe shop run by Mr Ryder. It was later taken by Mrs Friendship and changed to a small store.

I am relating what I was told as child. Apparently one of the founders of Lee Moor was a man called Phillips and he was one of my mum's ancestors. He was one of the people who first started using the clay to make pipes. I once found an old clay water pipe with Phillips embossed on it when I worked for ECLP, so maybe it's true.

When I left school at 16, I worked at ECLP as an apprentice fitter. I started in 1963, I think; I was qualified by the age of 21 and then worked with the company until 1975. I married a local girl, Marilyn Reid. Her dad was an electrical foreman at the clay refining plant in Plympton. All the time my ambition was to visit Africa – I think it was my Dad's stories, as he was stationed in Rhodesia during the war, so it became a major aiming point to me. The main mentors at work in Lee Moor were John Prout, Paul Selleck, Michael Quest, and Bill Kennard from No. 6 Sunderland Cottages; he was the foreman.

Donald Jones was the manager and I remember we pushed Phillip Jones (his son) through his office door on a trolley. Great glee. It knocked the door and the door frame into the office.

My fellow apprentices were Clive Friendship, Bob McNeil from Cornwood and Dave Andrew from Wotter. We used to play football at lunchtime. In the winter it was in the workshop, in the summer it was outside.

I remember breaking the sawmill window once, but no one told on me.

We also broke the time clock for coming to work and knocking off. I think it was Michael Howard who kicked the ball. Anyway, Mr Donald Jones came in after dinner (lunch) and we all started work again, a few hours later he looked around and said to Bill Kennard,

A carthorse ready to pull a carnival float, 1979.
(PHOTOGRAPH SUPPLIED BY DAVE ANDREW)

Lee Moor School, 1989.

A Christmas party in the old hall, c.1940.

Lee Moor Public Hall 1990.

'The clock's stopped'. He tried to wind it up with the key and discovered it was 'b*****d'. Needless to say, we all went on tiptoes chuckling for a few days.

On Thursdays Mr Quest from Plympton used to come to the village with his ice-cream van. We used to get paid on Thursdays (he wasn't daft), and one hot afternoon everyone had an ice-cream (a treat was the one with clotted cream) and we were sitting in the work-shop on our toolboxes. Mr Jones came in and said: 'What's going on here now? Anyone would think you were on Brighton Beach with the seagulls shitting all over you. Now back to work.'

I and Paul Selleck often used to have to work at Torycombe at the clay refining plant (Herreschoff). We used to walk down the hill in the morning carrying our tool bags and dinner and at 4.00p.m. walk back up to clock off.

It used to be a fitness match walking back. He was older and used to set the pace, but I always tried. When I started winning regularly we were moved to Lee Moor Pit. We were told it was one of the biggest open-cast pits in the world at that time. Try walking fast out of there at the end of the day. I did have a little advantage; I played football and didn't drink. He was my hero.

Anyway, where was I?

In 1975 I was married and living in Plympton with two small boys. It was a joint decision but we decided, Marilyn and I, to try to go to Africa. I answered an advert in a national paper and got a job in South Africa as a foreman fitter. We moved to South Africa in 1975. In late 1977 I got a job in Iran and went there for six months or so; they then had a revolution (remember the Ayatollah?) and I had to leave and returned to South Africa.

I worked for another year there and then got a job as a maintenance engineer in Botswana. I worked for that company for 19 years until 1998, then opened my own business (corrosion control, which is a fancy name for sand blasting and painting), and in 2007 am still doing it.

I don't regret a minute. Still living, not sick and ready to go the extra mile.

Lee Moor Public Hall

The following is a cutting from a local paper, c.1966:

Turkey Supper at Lee Moor The Christmas draw and turkey supper took place at Lee Moor Public Hall. Mr R. Tall (Chairman of Lee Moor Public Hall Central

Lee Moor WI perform 'It Ain't 'alf 'ot Mum' for their group meeting, c.1987. Included are Mary Williams, Mrs Friendship, Dorothy Friendship, Margaret Hugill, Pam May, Pauline Welch, Joan Fry, Mrs Sowden and Barbara Williams.

Board) welcomed the guests and paid tribute to the Lee Moor Carnival Queen, attendants and flower girls. Mr Albert Nayland and Mr Phillip Jones provided music for the dancing and games, which were organised by Mr K. Armistead.

The original Lee Moor Public Hall was built in 1936. It burned down on 2 June 1975. The cause of the fire was never discovered but it was thought it could have been a cigarette butt left burning (but see Phil Kerswell's memories at the beginning of this chapter, which may throw some light on the matter – DB). There had been a rehearsal that evening for a play which was to be produced by Rex Webber. Gordon May, the key-holder, went in just before going on night shift at the clay works to make sure everything was locked up and the lights were all switched off. The fire was discovered at around 11p.m. but by then it was too late and the hall was damaged beyond repair. The play was due to be performed on the Saturday of that same week. However ECLP, the clay company at that time, stepped in and saved the day by provided a marquee so the show could go on.

ECLP stands for English Clays, Lovering, Pochin. Weird but true. The company was formed in 1919 by the merger of West of England China Clay Co., Martyn Brothers and North Cornwall China Clays.

This was followed by the merger of English Clays with John Lovering and H.D. Pochin – ECLP & Co. for short. This was changed later to ECC International Ltd. The company was acquired by Imetal in 1999, which then changed its name to IMERYS, as it is today.

The hall was rebuilt in 1978/79 and the reopening was purposely arranged for 2 June 1979, the anniversary of its being burnt down. It was opened by Sir Allan Dalton, director of ECLP. Most of the materials were provided by ECLP and the work was mainly carried out by the villagers. Partying went on all day and evening for the opening.

The hall was, and is, used for all sorts of community activities and is quite an impressive hall for such a small community.

It is probably best well known for the pantomimes that used to be held there because the stage is as sophisticated and as well built as a small professional theatre.

Lee Moor Pantomime

Quite a number of pantomimes have been performed in the village over the years. However, it was a Madame Gow, an former professional actress and

Above: *A Lee Moor pantomime, though the production and the year are unknown.*

The cast of Sinbad.

Sinbad *again, with,* left to right, *?, Valerie Phillips, Gordon May, Ruth Howard, Dorothy Lillicrap, Bryan Pullyblank, Gordon Lillicrap, Michael Mottram.*

Unknown pantomime with, left to right: *Terry Legg, Bryan Pullyblank, Michael Mottram, Bert Ryder.*

believed to have been a real dame, who produced the first pantomime in the area, not in Lee Moor but in Wotter. It was *Cinderella*, and it received very little support. It was performed in the hall below the Methodist Chapel. Frank Grimes, who, it is thought, lived locally at the time and who was the managing director of ECLP, instigated and directed the first pantomime at Lee Moor Village Hall. Which pantomime it was we are not sure. All future pantomimes were then put on at Lee Moor. They continued to be organised by whoever was the chairperson of the Lee Moor committee at the time. Tom Andrews did all the painting of the scenery. The photographs come from different sources but were mainly contributed by Dave Andrew, Joyce Butcher and Bryan Pullyblank.

All the traditional pantomimes were performed, including the following;

1957 – Puss in Boots
1958 – Robinson Crusoe
1959 – Cinderella
1960 – Aladdin
1962 – Humpty Dumpty
1963 – Robin Hood and Babes in the Wood
1964 – Sleeping Beauty
1965 – Dick Whittington
1966 – Snow White and the Seven Dwarfs (Carol Martin, Lorna Lee)
1970 – Mother Goose

Unfortunately, as with a lot of voluntary organisations, without a driving force behind it the pantomime group eventually disbanded. There were only one or two pantomimes performed after the new hall was built because there was some sort of dispute between villagers, the cause of which seems

Robinson Crusoe, *1958.*

Cinderella, *1959.*

Cinderella, *1959*. Left to right: *Bryan Pullyblank, Lorna Lee, Deidre Phillips, Bill Broom, Les Turpin, Romaine Broome, George Douglas.*

Cinderella, *1959.*

Top and above: Aladdin, *1960*.

to be a dark secret which I am not privy to. Having myself been a member of a number of amateur theatre and pantomime groups I know the intrigue and machinations that can go on behind the scenes.

Joyce Butcher, née Lillicrap (aged 61)

I appeared in five pantomimes at Lee Moor from 1957 to 1962. We had a lot of fun, and we practised a lot! I was part of the chorus line. Dorothy Lillicrap used to teach us the dance routines; I think Ruth Howard helped as well. Mrs Jones and Mrs Phillips made a lot of the costumes, and we also had to take some home to finish

them off. However, some costumes were hired. The pantomime ran for a week and on the last night we had a party, and we used to get a bag of presents.

Mr Armistead was the producer and Tom Andrews (Wotter) painted the scenery; I think Venley Jones did the lighting. There were a lot of other people who helped but I can't remember all their names. The pantomimes were always very good and the hall was full every night.

In 1962 we had very heavy snow. I was working in Plymouth, and the bus only took passengers as far as Newnham, Plympton, so we had to walk the rest of the way. There were Nina Chambers, Ruth Howard and myself – I can't remember if there was anyone else. We

Unknown pantomime, 1970.

Mother Goose, *1972.*

Lee Moor Carnival, c.1960. The little girl in the front on the left is Elizabeth Walke, who lived on a farm in Goodameavy. Her sister is Susan Walke whose story appears in Chapter 2.

Lee Moor carnival, 1986.

Top and above: *Lee Moor carnival, 1987.*

walked up the lane and across the moor to Tiresome and up the hill to Lee Moor in the dark and it was blowing a blizzard. We walked holding on to each others' coats, one behind the other. As we started up the hill to Lee Moor we were met by Tony Squires, Michael Howard and some of the men from the panto. There was going to be a panto practice! We went into the hall, and had hot drinks. We were so cold – my trousers were frozen and stood up by themselves. There was no panto practice that evening!

I stayed with my sister and her children, who were living at Lee Moor. I had to stay at Lee Moor for several days before I could get home to Shaugh.

Lee Moor Carnival

The Lee Moor carnivals, a long-standing feature of village life, were, I'm told, also started by Frank Grimes. Every year large marquees were put up in the playing-fields for these occasions. These went on for a few years longer than the pantomimes but gradually fizzled out because newcomers to the village did not want to take part and had little interest. I'm not sure when they stopped.

A touching little story is told by Margaret Hugill (née May). She remembers an occasion when she was looking after a little girl called Donna who wanted to join in the carnival procession but had nothing prepared. Daphne (Margaret's sister) was looking after a lamb which had been abandoned by its mother, so they put Donna and the lamb in the parade as – guess what? – 'Mary had a little lamb'.

China Clay
written by Brian Pundsack (aged 62)

The following is an extract from a thesis on china clay written by Brian in 1964 as part of his third-year electronics apprenticeship at No. 1 Radio School, Royal Air Force Locking, Weston-super-Mare, when he was just 19 years old. Before joining the RAF he lived first at the Kiln at Shaugh Bridge and then in Wotter. I have extracted and précised the parts that I felt would be of most interest to the reader.

China Clay was first discovered in the South West in the early 1750s by a young chemist by the name of William Cookworthy, who was born in Kingsbridge in Devon. He had heard about a substance called china clay from travellers from the Far East. Being a chemist, he became interested and studied samples he was able to obtain. He learned how the substance was formed and how it was quarried. From this he realised there was a possibility of finding deposits in the West Country. He discovered deposits in Cornwall and a few years later deposits were found at Lee Moor. Most of the clay in the South West is to be found in Cornwall, but the deposits are small. The deposits in Devon, especially in Lee Moor, are much larger.

Although china clay is formed by the decomposition of feldspar. [Feldspar is the name given to rock-forming minerals, of which 60 per cent of the earth's crust is made –DB] *In granite, only a very small percentage of the granite is ever kaolinised. Dartmoor, the largest granite mass in the South West,*

Lee Moor clay works, 1989.

(PICTURE BY DAVE ANDREW)

Another view of Lee Moor clay works, 1989. (PICTURE BY DAVE ANDREW)

Water-pressure gun.

has not been extensively kaolinised. The southern edge of Dartmoor has a few deposits, the largest being in the Lee Moor–Shaugh Lake areas. This pit is the largest individual producer of basic raw material in the country [in 1964] and will probably continue to be so for many years.

The actual clay is extracted from the face by a strong blast of water from a high-pressure hose fed onto a special 'gun'. These guns are capable of pressure of 100ppsi. This jet drives out the clay from the face and into the clay-water stream.

All the impurities, including particles of rock of

A typical sand tip.

Channels at the clay works.

Clay works settling tanks.

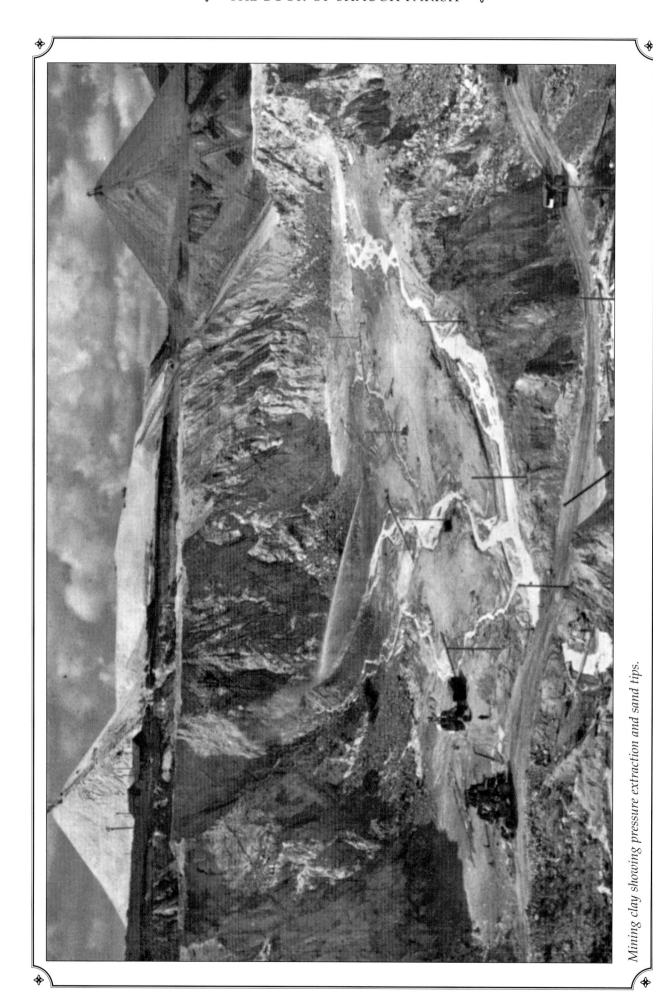

Mining clay showing pressure extraction and sand tips.

various sizes, run down the face to the bottom of the pit. The mixture is passed into special bins containing filters of various gauges. The sand and other particles are either manually or mechanically moved to adjoining bins built over the lower end of a rail line running from the bottom of the pit to the conical tip of the sand tip. The sand is loaded into wagons on the rails and hauled up the tip to be emptied.

After the clay stream has been filtered it is usually pumped to a higher level by a centrifugal pump. When it reaches the surface it is run into shallow parallel channels of such a length and gradient as to slow down the flow of liquid.

This allows the smaller particles, mainly quartz, to settle. The clay is then run into large pits to settle until it is creamy in texture.

It is then either left to settle or passed through presses to extract most of the water before going to the drying kilns. The standard drying kiln is a large floor space 200ft in length and 15ft wide (approximately 61m x 4.5m). Under the floor, or 'pan', of the kiln are flues through which hot air, heated at one end in a large furnace, passes through the length of the kiln to escape via a chimney at the other end [see Chapter 7 – DB]. The clay is left here until the water content has decreased to the require amount. It is then removed from the pan and stored in a 'linhay' [a lean-to shed with an open front – DB] until it is time for shipment.

China clay is used in the manufacture of fine porcelain but it is also used for cosmetics and in pharmaceutical products. For this it must be very pure and in a fine dust form. The raw china clay, after extraction and removal of basis impurities, is still not pure enough or white enough for these uses. Before it is allowed to settle and be dried it may go through other special purification plants. It may be bleached or other elements may be added to cause a catalytic effect. This does not actually affect the china clay but may combine with the impurities to make it easier to remove them.

Lee Moor Tramway

The following article was contributed by Dr Mark Howe. It explains how the clay produced at Lee Moor was transported. His very interesting and varied website can be viewed at www.hows.org.uk

The Lee Moor Tramway opened in about 1853 to carry china clay and other minerals from Lee Moor on the south side of Dartmoor to the quays in Plymouth, initially by horse, then by a mix of horse, gravity and steam power. It included a 2km long 1:11 counterbalanced cable incline through Cann Woods. You can see the bridge which carried the tramway over the road veering off to the NW at Plym Bridge; this is the major remaining feature of the incline.

The Lee Moor Tramway was used to transport china clay from the open-cast quarries at Lee Moor down to Plymouth for shipment. The LMT Co. owned two

Pecketts which were confined to the upper end of the line around the clay pits at Lee Moor and the first few miles to the Cann Incline. In the middle of the system was a rope-worked incline at Cann Woods where the wagons were lowered down the rope incline. The lower end of the system was horse worked right up until the end, and, unusually, made a crossing on the level of the Great Western main line just east of Laira engine shed, where horses were used to take the short clay trains on to the loading wharves at Cattedown in Plymouth. Traffic fizzled out after the war, when it was taken over by road transport and later on via a pipeline. The engines were stored at their shed at Torycombe for many years until the Lee Moor Tramway Society were given ownership of the No. 2 on the basis that they restored both No. 1 and No. 2. No. 2 was moved to Saltram in the mid-'70s, where it was expected to stay. No. 1 went to the Wheal Martyn mining museum near St Austell, where it remains to this day. The LMT system was 4ft6in gauge – known locally as 'Dartmoor Gauge'. Thus LMT No. 2 and its wagon will have to remain isolated from their standard gauge friends at Buckfastleigh.

The line had two inclines; the longer, at Cann Wood, was 1.25 miles long with a 1:11 gradient. It was a three track (middle rail common) with passing loop self-acting incline, the higher wagons being loaded thus heavier and their descent pulled up the empty lower wagons. This mechanism was controlled by a winding drum at the top which was braked to control the speed of the wagons.

The second incline was at Torycombe. Both of these were built in 1853 but had to be rebuilt in 1858 after lots of derailments. The Torycombe incline was again self acting, similar to the Can incline, but was a true single line with a passing loop. It was originally 29.5 chains long; when rebuilt it was 32.5 chains long, but the rise was still 300ft.

Arthur Diamond Selleck

This is the history of the Selleck family. It was written by Mr Arthur D. Selleck in 1970, when he would have been 79 years old. Born in 1891, he left school at age 13 and worked as a stoker in the clay drying kilns. He later trained as a blacksmith. This information was supplied by Malcolm Norman of Shaugh Prior. I have split the article into two, the first part being about living in Lee Moor and the second about the redevelopment of the clay industry in Wotter.

Lee Moor was a wonderful place to live in the early 1900s. Well over 100 children attended the Wesleyan Sunday school, with a staff of over 20 teachers taking bi-weekly turns, 10–11a.m. and 2.30–4.00p.m. Over 60 men could be seen at the morning service at 11 o'clock, and at the evening service often 150 people crowded into the little chapel to hear the preacher, who was usually a

Lee Moor, c.1926.

local; we had a regular minister about once a month. The choir stalls were always full and did they sing? James Bottes, Joe Manhire, George Selleck, Peter Phillips, Dick Short, Bob Gulley, John Selleck, Jack Tope in the bass section; James Bray, Chris Selleck, Jack Quest, John Lavers in the tenor section. Dear old Simian Lavers with his violin, and all those wonderful girls in the treble section. I was privileged at a very early age to sing in the alto section with Maude Manhire, Bessie Loram and others. What a wonderful time we had, Anniversary Sunday, then 'June Tae' (tea) on the Monday following. Sunday-school anniversary services were real festivals of praises – chapel packed to capacity, aisles, pulpit steps, choir steps, every inch of space occupied and often an overflow, scores of people too late to get inside. What a day! All the little 'tackers', boys and girls, the older lads and lasses and courting couples, parents and friends from the surrounding villages, all united to swell the glad song. Most of the parents contrived to fit us little ones out in new suits and dresses for that day. What a show! Picture hats for the girls and usually a wide, stiff collar stuck under chins for the boys. I remember we sang 'Brightly gleams our banner, pointing to the sky' (my collar certainly kept me looking in that direction). Another song which always lives with me was 'Love is the keynote, life is the song'. We always had the first prize 'Yorkshire Tune' each year. To the lasting credit of Mr and Mrs Bettes (choirmaster and organist respectively) that they produced a wonderful result in the training of children and choir. Then, with intense longing and excitement, we waited for the dawn of the next day. Anniversary Monday 'June Tae' was the great social event of the year. The children paraded through the village. Sitting after sitting of people would satisfy their appetites and tell their tales. Then

the younger ones would go down to the green (just above Torycombe Gate) to indulge in games – 'Kiss in the Ring' and 'Twos and Threes' were the first favourites, and many a romance had a beginning in the twilight of 'June Tae' day. We youngsters would strain our eyes to see the various arrivals, somebody from Torycombe would report that they had seen 'Cheap Jack', 'Penny Dip', 'Coconut shies' or 'Lyons' with his fruit stall – 'Billy Dip' in later years. Someone also with the 'Hobby Horses' – another with what was called 'Ladies' Teasers' – (tubes made of lead filled with water) with which the more adventurous 'roughs' of about nine would bombard the 'Kiss in the Ring', needless to say obstructing kissing operations. Sad to say it was a much depleted choir which gathered for the Monday evening service, especially in the soprano and alto section (I learned why as the years rolled on). These village Methodist tea drinks had to be experienced to be appreciated. How we looked forward to the time when we were old enough to be appointed by the Sunday-school committee to carry the hot water in those tin kettles around to the various tables at which Mrs or Miss Black, Lillicrap, Beadle, Bawgen, Lee, Colton, Loram, Manhire, Hore, Bray, Trethewy, Bettes, Phillips, Hoad, Elford, Jenkins, Lavers, Pillage, Quest, Ryan, Wilcox, Brooking, Luscombe, Osborne, Hicks, Hambly, Short, Serford, Mumford, Selleck, Tail, Roberts, McBean, Gill or Solomon were appointed to preside. These scenes were repeated in a lesser measure at Whitsun and Easter. 'Band of Hope' and 'Mission Band' teas, then Harvest Festival tea. What a glorious time was this. Saturday afternoon and evening; the fruit and vegetables, flowers, etc., would be received by the ladies, who had the knack of arranging so beautifully these gifts of our Heavenly Father. I still retain the memory of the aroma from the apples, pears and the other fruit and flowers. We lived very near heaven in those grand moments when those glorious traditional harvest hymns were sung. The full-throated resonant bass of Lee Moor choir in 'Come ye thankful people come', and the unison and heavenly harmony was something I do not expect to hear the like of this side of heaven. 'There were Giants' in those days in the pulpits of Methodism, not 'Preacherettes' giving 'Sermonettes' to 'Christianettes'. The Ebenezer circuit, of which Lee Moor was one of the outposts, could boast of wonderful men of God. Among the ministers outstanding were J.S. Hicks, C.T. Horn, Isaac Shimmin, Clifford Caddy, T. Caddy and many others. The local preachers, too, could hold boys' and girls' attention for 45 minutes to an hour. There were Isaac Foot senr, Henry Lawry, W.W. Lucas, James L. Nash, young 'Ikey' Foot, (now the Rt Hon Isaac Foot FC), Andrew Skardon, Messrs Skinner, J. Motley, and W. Gerry, who played the organ and also preached the sermon when Mrs Bettes was on holiday. Then the Lee Moor men – Lot Hoare, James Bettes, and Sam Trevan –that theological notable John Mumford – these men all by their faithful testimony helped to shape and direct under God the lives of others who followed in their steps.

'Ikey' Foot was always outstanding in insistence on the rightness of practical Christianity in national as well as local church life, and the story of Lee Moor would not be complete unless we recorded the impact of his preaching, speeches, lectures and example. When he preached we were uplifted spiritually. When he lectured we were benefited educationally. If he came to the district to speak on a political subject, even opponents were informed and edified. His lecture on Abraham Lincoln gave a distinct bias to my political thinking. The Boer War, which people thought started as a brief military operation but ended by being perilously near a major war, clouded our horizon. The political rendezvous in those days was the Co-op store. I remember when the newspapers arrived in the morning the older men would discuss the news and the respective merits and demerits of Daily Mercury or Morning News. Mr Harris, the Co-op manager, would act as chairman, while a wordy dual would proceed. Ben Trethewy, John Mumford, 'Ganger' Lillicrap and others would argue in favour of or against 'Imperialism'. The more adventurous spirits would run the risk of being called 'Pro-Boers' – we small boys were rather mystified when John H. Mumford was said to have abdicated piety in favour of political expediency, when he came out as a Liberal Imperialist. In the late 1890s Mr Reader Harris QC founded the Pentecostal League of Prayer. My father became the first leader of the 'Centre'. This was designed to be an interdenominational and international organisation with the object of strengthening spiritual life in all the churches. A centre was formed by something over a dozen praying Christians; the meeting of the league took place at 8a.m. on Sundays. This proved to be a great spiritual asset to our church and was certainly a spiritual 'Power House'.

I think of many outstanding Christians who were members of the Centre. One of the most memorable personalities was Jack Quest –'Click', as he was affectionately known. As a young man he was exceptionally strong and we small boys would wonder in real amazement at the weights he could lift. He was, however, destined to become one of the strongest examples of patience in sickness and adversity it was ever my privilege to witness. Early in his young manhood he developed a malady known as rheumatic chalk gout, which rendered him immobile. He lay like a human log for years with a face radiant with the joy of the Lord despite the excruciating pain he must have suffered. The chalk would ooze from every joint and knuckle in the form of a paste. Sometimes he would become unconscious as the brain was temporarily affected. I remember very vividly when my friend Frank Trethewy and I kept vigil through the night, how with the breaking of the dawn Jack roused suddenly from his state of coma and exclaimed: 'Frank, Arthur, rays from the son of righteousness and healing in his wings,' his face shining, his voice ringing with a heavenly ecstasy. He had a cheery word for everyone who came to see him. What an example of love and fortitude was his dear wife, who consistently and continually ministered to his needs and those of their three children – the effect of the impact of the life of Jack Quest on the spiritual life of many beside myself cannot be assessed by us.

As we have already stated, Lee Moor was then an isolated and self-contained community. Most of the workmen who lived in the twin villages of Lee Moor and Torycombe had their garden and allotment. Almost every householder kept pigs and poultry, many others kept a cow. The Dartmoor pony was also bred and kept in quite large numbers. Nearly everybody possessed a quite smart pony and turnout, either dogcart or jingle. In the old days it was quite an occasion when the farmers, led by farmer Tom Selleck, drove the ponies' 'drift' off Shaugh Moor to Noil Gate and then corralled them in one of the fields, where identification by the various owners took place.

Many scores of these animals were then driven by the Lee Moor owners back to the village for the branding mark to be applied to those which would be turned out on the moor again for breeding, some being retained for sale to dealers who came to buy them for use in the coal mines, etc.

August Bank Holiday was for many years a great day for Lee Moor. The local pony show took place in a field known as 'Company Park'. Classes for trotting, riding or driving ponies would be well filled and competition keen, and some outstanding animals were always to be seen, despite, of course, the fact that a fair proportion were something like 'Modbury Dancing', not very neat but strong. The musical programme on those occasions was provided by 'Tinker' Bray's band. The 'bombardon', as we were told it was called – that is the big bass – was blown by 'Tinker' himself. His son George on the cornet, his son Ned on the trombone – these were all outstanding performers. 'Tinker' could always be depended on to produce that deep, resonant bass note from the bowels of that weird instrument which had been bruised and dented over most of its surface, making any attempt at polishing impossible. Some of his Lee Moor critics insisted that he was sometimes a scat behind the rest. One of the most fascinating things to me was to watch Ned Bray blowing the trombone. How marvellously his cheeks would stretch – he seemed to distend his facial features to such an extent that we small boys would wonder when he would burst. But he would go on serenely producing those rolling notes. George Bray was a great hero because every small boy wanted to blow the cornet, and as we listened to him he always seemed to come in at the right times to save an awkward situation and to us he was only second to

Gabriel. There was, of course, quite a range of other players filling in the unity. There is a story told that on one of the very rare occasions that the band was engaged away from home to supply music at the celebrations at Plympton of the local Friendly Societies, the big drummer, Bill MacBean, who was small in stature, went on flogging the drum for quite a distance towards Plympton St Mary's Bridge while the band turned left at Dark Street Lane, but I could not vouch for the veracity of this report. However, 'Tinker' Bray's band was quite an institution and the band of the Royal Marines could not have been more important to us. 'Tinker' Bray and his family seemed to combine the attributes of both 'Tubal Cain' and 'Jubal Cain' (Genesis 4 v.21 & 22), as they were artificers in metals and also music makers.

Epilogue
The Saga of Writing The Book of Shaugh Parish

As I mentioned in the introduction, I had no intention of putting together a book entitled *The Book of Shaugh Parish*. This is the tale of the mishaps that happened on the way to the finished article. After deciding to put together the book I had thought of publishing it myself, but when I did the costings it was going to be over £1,000 to produce a couple of hundred books, £1,000 I didn't have to spare. Perhaps, I thought, I should knock the idea of a book on the head for the time being. It was then that Shaugh Prior Parish Council came to the rescue. A number of people on the Council had been very supportive and helpful. They suggested I contact Halsgrove Publishing, based in Somerset. After contacting them and discussing the matter they agreed to publish the book in their Community History series. Hallelujah!

So I had lots of memories, hundreds of photographs and an established and well regarded publisher; what could go wrong? Well, as it happens, quite a few things.

I decided to send a number of photographs to Halsgrove to ensure that the quality was sufficient. Shock, horror! Simon, the publisher, emailed me to inform me that most of the photographs I had sent them were unusable. What to do next? I had nearly 400 photographs ready, or so I thought, to be used in the book. Only one thing for it, I sent all of them to Simon. He replied in a few days with the grim news that all but 90 of the pictures were unusable and amongst the 90 were a lot of duplicates. I couldn't believe it. Most of the photographs were up on the website and they looked fine. What I wasn't aware of is that the standard for pictures on the internet is different from that required for the printed page. The internet is digital and uses pixels; the printing process uses dots per inch, or dpi for short. I won't bore you with the technical details because I don't quite understand them myself, but suffice to say that most of the pictures I had, had been supplied in digital format and been sent by email, which automatically reduces quality, or they had been scanned at a low resolution and so were unusable.

Now at this point I could have said, 'Oh Crikey!' or 'Dash it all!', and forgot the whole thing, and as I remember I did say something on those lines but more in the modern vernacular, if you get my drift. Thing is, when I start on a project I don't like quitting. So I didn't! If the photographs couldn't come to me then I would have to go and get them. After talking to Caroline Pitt, the Head of Shaugh Prior Primary

School, Elaine Smerdon the Chair of the Parish Council and Rachel Rayers, one of the organiser of the Parish Steering Committee's community day, I arranged to be at the school on a Friday afternoon in early February 2008, Lee Moor Public Hall on the Saturday and Shaugh Prior Recreation Hall on the Sunday, the aim being to encourage people with a connection to Shaugh Parish to bring along their photographs so that I could scan them direct into a computer. After being interviewed on a couple of radio programmes and having letters printed in the local papers publicising my visit, I was pretty confident that everything would go well. Problem sorted? Well, not quite. I had a lightweight scanner but I didn't have a laptop computer. No problem, I could borrow my wife's. No problem did I say? Try and get a piece of equipment a couple of years old to work with a new laptop fitted with the latest operating system. On second thought, don't bother. They are usually not compatible. The only thing to do was to buy a new laptop but with a compatible operating system. (Well, secretly I did want a laptop of my own – you know, boys' toys – so this was a good excuse.) With two weeks to go my new laptop arrived. Sleek and black. Switched it on... great! it works. Wait a minute, why won't the mouse work on it? Why can't I access the help files? Only thing for it was to contact the manufacturer's help line. Only trouble is the staff operating the help line are based in India and although I have no problems dealing with people from different races, sometimes we do have difficulties in making ourselves understood. Still, Reeta and I did build up quite a bond in the three hours we spent on the telephone to each other. She made every effort to sort out the problem. Did she? Unfortunately not. In the end it was decided that there was a problem with the motherboard and it would have to be replaced.

The engineer came five days later and replaced the motherboard and got the machine working sweet as a nut. I installed all the software I needed, including the software to operate the scanner. Tested it. Hooray! everything works fine, ready to go, and go I did, but not before making a disc of all the photographs of the parish I had so we could have a slideshow. I arrived at the school in time to be treated to school dinner. Long time since I had one of those at Shaugh, to be precise 51 years. How time flies. After giving a little talk to some of the children about life at Shaugh Bridge in the '50s people began to arrive.

I plug my scanner into the laptop and guess what? Yes, you've got it. The scanner won't work. The computer won't recognise it and is asking for the drivers. But I installed the drivers, you stupid machine (can't swear in front of the children). Luckily we are in the IT suite at the school and can use one of the school's scanners, but not before a couple of the children and I spend a fraught 15 minutes trying to work out how to reset the dpi. Success at last! Whilst I spend the afternoon reminiscing with people who attended the school as long ago as I did, two little pupils of the school aged nine take over the task of scanning the photographs and operating the computer. Isn't it wonderful how these little children are at home in the computer age? All in all a successful day. I visit my niece Sarah that evening; she is a bit of a whiz with computers. She plugs the scanner into my laptop and it works straight away. Cursed thing, why didn't it work for me this afternoon? Nobody knows.

Saturday dawns fine and I go to the bathroom to do my ablutions. Oh no! I've forgotten my electric razor. But never fear, there in the bottom of my toilet bag is a wet razor. How long it has been there I don't know. What I do know is that I have never used it, so it should be nice and sharp. I don't have any shaving soap so I make do with washing soap. The razor slides smoothly over my chin, but, wait a minute, that's not a very close shave, I can still feel the bristles. Ah, there's the problem. I've got the head fitted on the wrong way. Soon fix that and start again. Now I know what you are thinking – I bet he cut his face to ribbons. Well, you would be wrong. Smooth as a baby's bum. Not a mark. Not a blemish. Not yet, that is! I decide to put on some very expensive aftershave balm that my wife bought me for Christmas and off I go to Lee Moor Hall. Rachel has brought along a laptop and projector so we can run the slideshow from the disc of pictures I have brought along. I need my laptop for use with the scanner so I cand copy people's photographs. After a bit of experimentation we finally get Rachel's laptop and projector set up and working. Slip in the disc, press play and Hey Presto! We are off and running. Hang on a minute, the pictures are all funny. They look like colourful negatives. We try the disc in my laptop and it works fine. We try the spare disc. Same result. By coincidence the laptops are the same make, the operating systems are the same, and they should work the same. But they don't. The wonders of technology! Rachel suggests we run the projector and slideshow from my computer for the time being. That works great. I decide to see whether my computer is powerful enough to run the projector and the scanner together. It is. Problem solved.

By mid morning I feel the call of nature and visit the gents. While washing my hands I glance into the mirror. Hells Bells, what's happened? My face is covered in large red blotches. Luckily there is a St John Ambulance attendant on hand to have a look. He reckons I have taken a layer of skin off and putting on the balm has aggravated the situation and inflamed the next skin layer. By now my face is burning, not just because of the blotches but because of the embarrassment as well. A man of my age with such tender skin. Ah well, I suppose I could have paid a small fortune to go to a beauty parlour and have a skin peel.

By the following morning the inflammation had to a degree subsided but my face was still a little sore, so I refrained from shaving. It was a beautiful morning so I went to Shaugh Bridge to take more photographs. Just before noon I went up to the White Thorn to meet my family and pick up the key to Shaugh Public Hall from Will, the landlord. I was feeling good. I'd had a lovely morning. I had the key to the hall and I was looking forward to a nice Sunday lunch with my sister, et al. Nothing could go wrong. Or could it? I was chatting to Will when a lady came up to the bar and asked for the key to the hall. Will told her I had it. She said she needed it to prepare for a children's party. Thinking they were preparing for another day I handed over the key, but on further delving it became obvious that the children's party was planned for later that day at the same time as I was booked in. The hall had been double booked! I went down to the hall to meet the people who were holding the party. There followed a discussion about who had booked the hall first, and we then tried to contact the person who had taken the bookings, but to no avail; they weren't in. There then followed a fraught 15 minutes in which we discussed how we were going to work this out. In the end we agreed that I would use the stage for a slideshow and to talk to the people who were coming along and the children would use the main part of the hall for their party. It's fair to say that in the circumstances it worked quite well. The children enjoyed their party and for the next few hours, apart from the noise level being raised by screaming happy children, the day was trouble free.

From the foregoing you will have realised by now that the preparation of this book has not been without its traumas and upsets, but nothing too serious, thankfully. Would I do it again? Are you mad? Of course I wouldn't! Before I started this project I had a full head of black hair and an unlined face. Now most of the hair is gone and what is left is white. My face has more lines than a schoolboy kept in detention. Well, perhaps I do exaggerate a bit. As I'm always being reminded by my wife, after every play I write or direct I always get grumpy and swear I will never do it again, but within a few weeks I'm ready to start all over again.

What comes next I wonder? Shaugh the play? Shaugh the musical? Now I really am getting carried away!

Subscribers

Mr and Mrs A Abbott-Creber, Wotter, Devon

Hazel Adams (née Damerell)

Ron Ayers, Devonport

Doris Emily Baskerville

Melvyn E. Blackmore, Estover, Plymouth

Roger O. Blackmore, Brixton, Plymouth

Jean Body (née Damerell), Saltash, Cornwall

Brian and Margaret Brazier, Shaugh Prior

Mr and Mrs R. Bryan

K. J. Burrow, Bucks Cross, Devon

Joyce and Kelvin Butcher, Cornwood, Devon

James and Geneva Chapple, Kansas, USA

Kenneth Clarke, Bideford, Devon

Malcolm Clarke, Roborough, Devon

The Comptons, from Shaugh Prior

Mr D. and Mrs B. Coombes, Shaugh Prior

Tim Damerell, Wotter, Shaugh Prior Parish

Carol Damerell, Plympton, Devon

Debbie Davey, Cheltenham (formerly of Lee Moor)

Patricia Dimmick, Plympton, Devon

Rosemarie Dimmick, Wotter, Devon

Benjamin Shaun Earl, Plymouth

Martha Loveday Elder, Buxton

Beatrice Valentine Elder, Buxton

Robert Elder, Plymouth

Dolly Elford

Violet W. Faulkner, Shaugh Parish, Devon

Mrs June Fellows, Formerly of Broadoaks, Lee Moor

Della (née Munro) and Nigel, Mark and Megan
  Fellows, "Bijoro" Lee Moor

Stan Finnemore, Shaugh Prior, Devon

Sam Fry, Lee Moor, Devon

Laurence Gibson, Stowe, Bucks

John Giles, Shaugh Parish, Devon

Archie L. Haill, Shaugh Prior, Devon

Peter Hallam, Ex China Clay Works

Carroll and Verna Harder, Kansas, USA

Teresa Harvey, Shaugh Parish, Devon

Mrs Heather Harvey, "Bijoro" Lee Moor
  (Formerly of Coldstone)

Nicola Harvey,

Mrs Sally J. Hirst, née Olver, Wotter, Devon

Martin Hugill, Plympton (formerly of Lee Moor)

Terry Ireland, Ivybridge, Devon

Desmond Jarvis, Barry, Wales

Iza and Charles Jellyman

Christopher Jones, Ontario, Canada

Mr Sidney C. Jones, Shaugh Prior, Devon

Esther Jones (née Tucker) formerly Jutson,
  Shaugh Parish, Devon

Colin Jutson, Shaugh Parish, Devon

John K. Kingwell, Shaugh Parish, Devon

Susan Lang, Plymstock, PlymouthS. Lapthorn
  (née Skelley), Born Wotter

Robert Lee, Weymouth

John Lee, Lee Moor

Tommy and Marion Legg, formerly of Wotter,
  Plymouth, Devon

Roy Lillicrap, Plympton

Susan Lyons (née Walke), Bedfordshire

Brian Maddock, Worthing, West Sussex

Kathryn Malachowski, USA

Caroline Martin

Richard Martin

Patrick and Angela Martin, Shaugh Prior

Dorothy May

Gordon May

John May

Rosalind May, New Brunswick, Canada

Mr and Mrs Richard May and Nick, Hunsdon Road,
  Westlake, Devon

Mr and Mrs Robin May, Victoria and William,
  Birchland Farm, Sparkwell, Devon

Barbara Y. McIntosh, Shaugh Parish, Devon

John and Linda Milford, Shaugh Prior

Neil and Julie Morton, Wotter, Devon

Philip and Valerie Munro, Formerly of Coldstone

Graham John Naylor, Plymouth, Devon

Gary Nicholson, Plympton, Devon

Malcolm Norman, of Huxton Farm

Mrs Betty Norton (née Pullyblank),
  Tavistock, Devon

Frances Oliver, Old Windsor, Berks

Mr and Mrs D Parker, Lee Moor, Devon

Mavis Parr, Fleet, Hampshire

Sydney Roger Parsons, Jarrahdale,
  Western Australia

Sue Pascoe, Lee Moor

Linda and Carole Peters, Shaugh Bridge Killen

Miss C Pitt, Horrabridge, Devon

Brian Pundsack, Shaugh Prior

Damon Ralph

Rachel Rayers, Parishioner

Ken Rickard, Lydford, Devon

Rob Hubble and Stella Tracey, Shaugh Prior

Wilford Roberts, Shaugh Parish, Devon

Margaret Roberts, Shaugh Prior, Devon

Susan Robinson, Nova Scotia, Canada

Mrs Sheila Rogerson, Shaugh Parish, Devon

Carol Rowe, Redruth

Dawn Rowland, Elfordleigh, Plympton

Shaugh Prior Primary School, Shaugh Prior, Devon

Ronald A. Skelley, Wotter, Shaugh Parish

Marilyn and John Small, Lee Moor

Lorna, George and David Small, Sparkwell

Jack Small

Steven Smerdon

Nina and Tony Squires

The Stickland Family, Shaugh Bridge

Janet and John Stitson, Plymouth

Robert W. Stokes, Shaugh Prior

Pauline Talbot, Crows Nest, Cornwall

Susan Teague, St Austell

The McIntosh Family, Lee Moor

Mr Mark Thomas, Shaugh Mill

Mr Andrew Thomas, Shaugh Mill

Mrs J. Torr (née Roberts), Woodford, Plympton

Vanessa Tyler, Shaugh Parish, Devon

David Tyrrell, Horrabridge, formally of Wotter

Michael L. Waldron, North Wales

Mrs B. Walke, Horrabridge, Devon

Edna Walker (née Damerell), Ivybridge, Devon

Jennifer M. Wall, Shaugh Parish, Devon

Dr L.H. Walter, Shaugh Bridge

Ida M. Warn (née Olver), Shaugh Parish

Rex H. Webber, Lee Moor, Devon

Pauline Welch

Dr. J Winter, Shaugh Parish, Devon